PRAISE F

LEADERSHIP EXPLOSION

"If your groups need more leaders, this book is for you! Dr. Comiskey demonstrates how effective churches develop leaders. Then he shows you how to do the same by outlining the principles of leadership development that will work in any church. This book will revolutionize your future ministry."

C. PETER WAGNER
Chancellor, Wagner Leadership Institute

"Once again, Joel Comiskey has provided a book that answers the questions of those in the cell church movement. I read the manuscript with pen in hand, underlining so many sentences that few were left untouched! This book is an excellent reference for cell leaders and might well be incorporated into their ongoing training."

RALPH W. NEIGHBOUR, JR.
Founder, TOUCH Outreach Ministries

"Many thanks to Comiskey for a helpful and practical book. Many church growth strategies work in the short run, but only leadership multiplication creates ongoing kingdom expansion. This book communicates biblical, proven and effective principles. Eat this book! Let it shape your heart, your vision and your strategy."

JIM EGLI
Author, Pastor, and TOUCH Trainer

LEADERSHIP EXPLOSION

LEADERSHIP EXPLOSION

MULTIPLYING CELL GROUP LEADERS TO REAP THE HARVEST

JOEL COMISKEY

TOUCH PUBLICATIONS

Houston, Texas, U.S.A.

Published by TOUCH Publications
10055 Regal Row, Suite 180
Houston, Texas, 77040, U.S.A.
(713) 896-7478 • Fax (713) 896-1874

Cover design by Don Bleyl
Text design by Rick Chandler

International Standard Book Number: 1-880828-23-5

TOUCH Publications is the book-publishing division
of TOUCH Outreach Ministries, a resource and consulting
ministry for churches with a vision for cell-based local
church structure.

Find us on the World Wide Web at
http://www.cellgrouppeople.com

ACKNOWLEDGMENTS

This book has taken years to research, write, edit, perfect, edit, perfect, edit . . . and finally see light. In the long process, many hands and eyes have handled and contributed to the final work. Several people deserve special recognition.

First, I want to thank Greg Collard, a teacher at the Alliance Academy in Quito, Ecuador, for spending many hours editing the original form of this book. Although Greg is well-known for his editing expertise, he refused any remuneration for his work, insisting that he was doing it for the Lord. Second, I want to thank my editor, Scott Boren, for offering invaluable insight and suggestions throughout the long journey that has now finally ended in publication. Finally, I want to thank my wife, Celyce, for her continual encouragement and wise counsel along the way.

CONTENTS

FOREWORD

While I was conducting the 20/20 Vision Seminar on how to have successful small groups, an enthusiastic young pastor shared how he had discovered to his surprise that lots of people wanted to be in small groups. He then told me that his only limitation was developing and producing new leaders.

I believe that my friend, Joel Comiskey, who has committed his life to helping churches all over the world in cell ministries, is giving us what we need help with in this book. It scratches where we all itch.

This book focuses on how a church can develop leaders effectively in and through small groups. It highlights how small groups are breeding grounds for developing leaders.

Joel has researched effective cell churches around the world and created case studies of their leadership development methods. With these insights you can learn from the most effective cell church leaders.

From 1972 to 1995 I had the joy of pioneering what many have called one of the most effective small group systems in North America. We experienced big things in small groups. Thousands were brought to Christ and then effectively discipled and cared for in small groups. In retrospect, the one thing that we did that was the most outstanding was develop hundreds of leaders. If you build leaders, they will build cell groups and through them, the church.

Peter Drucker taught that to be an effective leader you don't have to do everything right, you have to do the right things. Along with Joel, I am absolutely convinced that the right thing to do is develop leaders through cell ministry.

Nothing could be more right for those who want to be effective in reaching people and building churches than reading this book and learning how better to develop your leaders through cell ministry.

If you catch what is taught in this timely book on developing leaders through the cell system, your groups will multiply and reach many more people because you will have the leaders to build new groups. Furthermore, you will produce strong leaders who will build your church into the future.

Dale E. Galloway
The Beeson International Center
Wilmore, KY

INTRODUCTION
"WE NEED MORE LEADERS"

I recently saw *The Harvest,* a video which tells the story of a farm boy who lost his father. The farmer had impressed upon his son the importance of harvest time. When the boy was 12 his father died, right before the grain harvest. Grief struck the boy, and he was sickened by the thought of a ripening harvest with no one to reap it. He knew he could not reap it by himself. As the hot sun beat down, the fear of losing the harvest overwhelmed him.

One afternoon a sound in the distance pierced his anxiety. He looked up to see dozens of tractors approaching the farm. Friends and neighbors had gathered together to reap the harvest. It was their way of expressing appreciation for their deceased friend. In one day, they reaped the entire harvest.

Today, we're seeing the greatest harvest of souls in Christian history. This is the good news. The bad news however is that much of the harvest is not completed and is often left to spoil. The harvest is ready but workers are needed to bring the harvest in successfully. When Jesus saw multitudes swarming around him, he said to his disciples, "Do you not say, 'Four months more and then the harvest'? I tell you, open your eyes and look at the fields! They are ripe for harvest" (John 4:35). Jesus told the church to make disciples, not to gather multitudes. If the church is going to reap the harvest today, it must make disciples who are willing to lead others and willing to influence others for the sake of Christ. They must take the risk to lead those who seek Christ.

So often we see the multitudes but don't contemplate their awful state. Jesus did more than analyze the condition of the lost. He had compassion on them because ". . . they were harassed and helpless, like sheep without a shepherd" (Mt. 9:36). This compassion stirred Christ to exhort his followers to, ". . . Ask the Lord of the harvest, therefore, to send out workers into his harvest field" (Mt. 9:36-38). We can't reap the harvest alone. We need help. This book is about raising up leaders to reap the harvest.

I've researched small groups around the world. Here's what I've discovered: Small groups are not the answer. In fact, there is danger in thinking that small groups are the answer. Small groups come and go; they rise and fall over time. Unless small group members are converted into small group leaders, little long-term fruit remains.

Churches do not reap the harvest because they have small groups. They reap the harvest because they have harvest workers. Churches that have no plan to develop leaders have, by default, planned to lose the harvest.

"The growth of the cell movement is based on raising up leaders from within. The highest priority of the cell leader is to identify prospective interns and begin the mentoring process."[1] With this quote, Gwynn Lewis pinpoints the purpose of this book. Cell leaders are not called primarily to form and sustain cell groups; their primary job is to find, train, and release new leadership.[2] Jim Egli expands on this point: "The cell model is not a small-group strategy; it is a leadership strategy. The focus is not to start home groups but to equip an expanding number of caring leaders. If you succeed at this, your church will flourish."[3]

Some people react negatively to the word *leader* because of its connotations of position and power. For example, in some cultures, a leader is a person who controls and dominates. Others imagine that a Christian leader must hold an official position in the church. A new consensus, however, has developed that defines the word *leader* in one word: influence.[4] When I use the word *leader* in this book, I'm referring to a person who exercises his or her God-given capacity to *influence* a specific group of God's people toward God's purposes for the group."[5] In this book, my use of the word leader implies such Biblical words as *servant, disciple, or harvest worker.*

I hope that by reading this book, you will obtain small group leadership eyes, so that you can see your congregation in a new light. What a difference it made in my church when we began to see people with leadership eyes! For years we focused primarily on Sunday morning attendance. We considered ourselves successful because we filled the pews on Sunday morning. If attendance dipped, we urgently planned special Sunday events to reverse the downward trend. Today, we still long for multitudes on Sunday morning, but we now recognize that God's concept of church is more than just the people who attend on Sunday morning. Now we prioritize the converting of Sunday worshippers into cell leaders who are reaching their neighbors for Christ. Our yearly goal is how many new cell groups we're going to start. We've discovered the secret weapon of the cell church: developing an army of committed cell leaders to reap the harvest.

This book draws principles from each of the most prominent cell churches around the world, so that you can apply what best fits your present needs. I have visited and studied fast growing cell churches which include but are not limited to:

- Bethany World Prayer Center in Baker, LA
- Yoido Full Gospel Church in Seoul, Korea
- International Charismatic Mission in Bogota, Colombia
- The Christian Center of Guayaquil in Quayaquil, Ecuador
- Elim Church in San Salvador, El Salvador
- Faith Community Baptist Church in Singapore
- Love Alive Church in Tegucigalpa, Honduras
- Living Water Church in Lima, Peru

I have also studied many cell leadership training models in the United States that have contributed to the conclusion of this book.

As you read what other cell churches are doing, remember the church growth axiom: "Don't follow methods; extract the underlying principles from the methods and apply them to your situation." Your circumstances are unique. The methods practiced in other churches won't fully meet your needs. The principles behind those methods, however, are transferable to any situation, including your own. If you capture the importance of cell leadership development and gain insight into how to do it, this book will have served its purpose.

FOUNDATIONS FOR DEVELOPING CELL LEADERS

1

BARRIERS TO
DEVELOPING LEADERS

"Our leaders are tired," the pastor said to me. "They've been leading small groups for some time now, and they want a break. What should I tell them?" Without waiting for my reply, he tested me with his own answers, "Maybe I should just let them rest for awhile; maybe I should open and close the groups each semester. What should we do differently?"

I noticed that his church was already full of activity, and that new programs would soon be added to the agenda. Hoping for a miracle answer, he attended my cell seminar in which I focused on breaking down the leadership barrier. I taught those attending how to develop new workers and how to keep their present leadership healthy. He thanked me profusely after the seminar, which had touched a vital chord in his own life and ministry. This pastor, like the myriads before him, was face to face with the leadership barrier.

Churches rise or fall on available leadership. One of the reasons that church attendance is at an all-time low is the lack of leadership.[1] Unless you have a clear plan to develop church attendees into church leaders, the ebb and flow of church attendance will continue to drop. Why is there such a dearth of lay leadership? Here are a few reasons:

TIME DRAIN

"I'm overloaded at work, pastor." "Maybe next year I can get involved in the church." Have you heard these excuses? More and more church members insist that they have no time for leadership involvement. The time drain barrier tops the list.

Recent studies indicate that Americans work the longest hours in the industrialized world — nearly 2000 hours per year. Between 1977 and 1997, the average workweek among salaried Americans lengthened from 43 to 47 hours. Over the same years, the number of workers putting in 50 or more hours a week jumped from 24 percent to 37 percent. Scarcely a decade ago, Americans were horrified with the work habits of the Japanese. Now, according to a recent report of the International Labor Organization, the United States has passed Japan to become the longest-working nation in the world.[2] The average American works eight weeks more per year than the average western European; the same report says that Americans run a risk of burning out.[3]

Church members know that in order to keep their jobs they must work the extra hours. The load of ministry, therefore, falls upon the church pastor. Church work is volunteer work, and with the precious time that we possess, it's important to choose where and how to spend it. In an increasingly secular society, many people scratch church work off their list of "things to do." Admittedly, this is a big hurdle for pastors to overcome, but solutions abound.

CHURCH ATTENDANCE FOCUS

I believe in church growth. My core church philosophy centers on church growth theory, and I believe that God wants His church to grow in both quality and quantity. If the major focus, however, is how many people attend on Sunday morning, a leadership void can occur.

When a church focuses primarily on Sunday morning attendance, the people feel like they've fulfilled their purpose simply by showing up on Sunday. The goal is Sunday attendance and members hear this in many subtle ways. A church, without knowing it, can produce a grand multitude that keeps shifting as people shuffle in and out. The back door is often as large as the front door and in the meantime, few leaders are developed.

Peter is a perfect example of this malady. He came to our church after many years in a denominational church that emphasized the Sunday morning service. God had miraculously saved Peter from a life of wild living, but the church found little use for him. When he came to us, we immediately saw his potential. We asked him to enter the training track to eventually become a cell leader. In the meantime, one of our youth cell leaders began leading a group in Peter's home. We didn't view Peter as an attendee in our church. Instead, we saw him as a potential leader in the harvest and even a future leader of leaders.

From 1991 to 1997, we prioritized Sunday morning attendance and grew each year. In 1997, however, we performed house cleaning. We examined the inner workings of our church and didn't like what we found. An exceedingly small percentage of the Sunday worshippers actually participated in prayer, training, and small groups. Our unbalanced Sunday morning emphasis produced few leaders. We were doing all the work and seeing little fruit.

When your church begins to focus on developing leaders, those attending Sunday worship will catch a greater vision and will become fishers of men, thus reaching out to others. The result is church growth, the very thing that pastors desire. With our new emphasis on producing leaders, we're experiencing the best of both worlds. We're experiencing record levels of attendance and giving, but our focus is on leadership development. We have our cake and we're eating it too.

ACADEMIC TRAINING MINDSET

Many church leaders know how to develop teachers but not leaders. Education, not leadership, dominates the agenda. The first volunteer position to fill is the Sunday school teacher. When the Sunday school spots are occupied, the pastor might look for committed people to lead other church programs, but the creative, energetic lay person is stymied. Since few leadership positions exist, those aspiring to lead feel frustrated.

Leadership is more than volunteering to complete a task in the church. Leaders lead people. A leader with no one following is only going for a walk. A teacher can impart information and a department head can administrate a program, but leaders minister to others and influence their lives. They get involved in the nitty-gritty details of other people. This requires a shift from academic training to leadership training.   P.M.A.D.

FAULTY LEADERSHIP TRAINING

Christian education in many churches is not conducive for mobilizing lay leadership. The goal of training is unclear and the training process is even fuzzier. Everyone is encouraged to enter the classes, but few know what they are being trained to do. The hope is that leaders will develop by themselves. This barrier is often imperceptible. "After all," many pastors muse, "I have many leaders in my church." When you look closer, you'll often discover self-made leaders who were developed outside the church.

The phrase "general education" characterizes the training in most churches. The goal is often to prepare a person to live the Christian life, rather than to lead a group of a people. I'm in no way criticizing general education. My love for learning propelled me to acquire a Ph.D. Lifetime learning is, in fact, a highly valued leadership trait. Churches, however, are uniquely positioned to help exercise the muscles of the lifetime learners and to transfer head knowledge to the feet. Effective leaders come down from the lofty tower and succeed in the trenches, where the battle for souls is won or lost.

Yet, even when a person does feel prepared, there's often a lack of available openings for service. For these reasons and others, a few key people do all the work. Researchers have repeatedly discovered that in most churches, 10% of the people do 90% of the work.

INABILITY TO MENTOR OTHERS

Studies show that the North American culture is the most individualistic in the entire world.[4] This mindset doesn't encourage a humble posture of learning and helping others in a mentoring relationship. Mentoring others, a relational experience through which one person empowers another by sharing God-given resources, is not common in our society.[5] Most of us learn new truth by osmosis — lots of knowledge making its way through a wide variety of sources.

Gratefully, others have worked their way through my shell and helped mentor me. I was especially privileged to work under Pastor Henry Alexander, a mentoring pastor. He took me under his wings and imparted years of experience to me. As I looked down upon Henry at his funeral, I thanked God for the resources he poured into my life. I said to the crowded church that morning, "Pastor Henry was a spiritual father to me." More than anything else, he was there for me.

Very few mentor like Pastor Henry. I worked under one pastor who developed few relationships with others (including myself), wore an attitude of superiority (rather than the attitude of a learner) and was eventually asked to leave the church. The failure to mentor potential leaders has erected a huge leadership barrier in the church today.

THEOLOGY OF PRIESTHOOD OF BELIEVERS

Pastoral theology in the traditional Bible school or seminary focuses primarily on what the pastor should do. To be honest, I fell in love with this view of the pastor. I romanticized the pastor's role, secretly reveling in how many people would be dependent on me in my future ministry. In numerous courses on pastoral theology, I was taught how to visit, preach, marry, bury, administer, evangelize and all the other pastoral jobs. The clear message that I received was that everything depended on me, the senior pastor.

Perhaps seminaries simply reflect what most churches expect: that the pastor performs and makes it all happen. After all, he's getting paid for it. The suggestion that members should do the work of the ministry is offensive to some. The expectations of church members, along with traditional pastoral training, erect a high leadership barrier.

While the church has done a good job of training people to go directly to God, by and large, it has failed to train people to minister to others. The pastor is still considered the priest, the only one fit to minister. This barrier, tied in with lack of mentoring, produces a church of spectators who watch the pastoral performance each Sunday. Long accustomed to sit and soak, the "sermon tasters" in many churches become experts in critiquing the pastor and grumbling when their needs aren't met. How far have we fallen from New Testament Christianity of Peter's day when he depicted the church as ". . . a chosen people, a royal priesthood, a holy nation, a people belonging to God" (1 Peter 2:6).

Just what is the role of the pastor? To care for those who attend church each week? To offer services to those who pay tithes? This goes to the heart of the issue and the major reason for writing this book. Maybe you are reading this book as a frustrated pastor looking for answers. You've grown weary with the traditional role of pastor. You feel locked in a box, playing a tit-for-tat relationship with church members and church boards. This book will suggest a reexamination of Scripture concerning the role of the pastor. Theology must breed practice, not vice versa. Many of the problems in today's church stem from faulty theology.

How Small Groups Break Barriers

Small group ministry doesn't provide the cure-all for all the problems in the local church. It does, however, satisfy several key needs. First, it provides a significant role for lay people. As Carl George says, "I'm convinced that lay people take ministry to a limited size group so seriously that they prefer a role in cell leadership to most any other office or honorific title in a church"[6] Small group ministry prepares a person to pastor, evangelize, administrate, care for others, and use his or her gifts and talents. Lay people feel like they're doing something significant.

Second, small group ministry is the perfect training ground for future leaders in the church. Small groups have correctly been called *leader breeders*. People learn to labor. They are equipped for ministry. They are encouraged to exercise their gifts. They develop vision. Ultimately, they become leaders. I started my ministry in a small group. I learned to lead, teach, exhort, administer and above all, pastor a small group of people. Potential leaders spread their wings in a small group atmosphere. They take baby steps by leading a group component — worship, prayer, and eventually the small group lesson. Would-be leaders learn through an incremental process of doing and learning.

Third, small group ministry makes the pastor's job easier. Because small group leaders assume a pastoral role, they do the work of the ministry and truly minister to the needs of the congregation as well as reach out to non-Christians. We find parallels here with the apostles and the needs of the early church. When the Grecian Jews complained against the Hebraic Jews because their widows were being overlooked in the daily distribution of food, the early church gathered all the disciples together and said, "It would not be right for us to neglect the ministry of the word of God in order to wait on tables. Brothers, choose seven men from among you who are known to be full of the Spirit and wisdom. We will turn this responsibility over to them and will give our attention to prayer and the ministry of the word" (Acts 6:1-4).

Placing people into small groups does not guarantee leadership development. It's only the beginning. First, you must see your people as God does.

2

DEVELOPING
EVERYONE

A study of 300 highly successful people such as Franklin Roosevelt, Helen Keller, Winston Churchill, Albert Schweitzer, Mahatma Gandhi, and Albert Einstein revealed that one-fourth had handicaps such as blindness, deafness, or crippled limbs. Three-fourths had either been born in poverty, come from broken homes, or from exceedingly tense or disturbed situations. [1]

Sometimes we fail to see emerging leadership because we are looking for the wrong things. We often look for those who mesh with our personality but pass over those who follow a different drummer.

Samuel misjudged the Lord's choice for the second king of Israel because he focused on height and stature: "Samuel saw Eliab and thought, 'Surely the LORD's anointed stands here before the LORD.' But the LORD said to Samuel, 'Do not consider his appearance or his height, for I have rejected him. The LORD does not look at the things man looks at. Man looks at the outward appearance, but the LORD looks at the heart'" (1 Samuel 16:6-7).

Jesse was just as surprised that his older children were not elected. He had not even considered inviting his shepherd boy David to the ceremony. But even though David was a "ruddy" young boy, ". . . the LORD said, 'Rise and anoint him; he is the one!'" (1 Samuel 16:11-12).

God tends to use the "ruddy, young boys" that are fully committed to him. Our tendency is to hang educational nooses around budding leaders. Yet the harvest is so plentiful and the laborers are so few that God would have us look at all leadership possibilities around us.

CHRIST'S CHOICE OF THE 12

It's surprising that Jesus did not choose key, prominent men to form part of His 12. None of Christ's disciples occupied important positions in the synagogue, nor did any of them belong to the Levitical priesthood. Rather, they were common laboring men with no professional training, no academic degrees, and no source of inherited wealth. Most were raised in the poor part of the country. They were impulsive, temperamental, and easily offended. Jesus broke through the barriers that separated the clean and unclean, the obedient and sinful. He summoned the fisherman as well as the tax collector and zealot. Jesus saw hidden potential in them. He detected a teachable spirit, honesty, and a willingness to learn. They possessed a hunger for God, a sincerity to look beyond the religious hypocrisy of their day, and they were looking for someone to lead them to salvation. In calling the despised to Himself, in sitting down to a meal with sinners, in initiating the restoration of a Samaritan woman, Jesus demonstrated that even these people were welcomed into the kingdom of God.

A Word to Pastors

Pastor, most of the leadership problems can be solved if you are willing to develop the lay people within your own congregation. True, this will require that you open your heart to a broader spectrum of lay people in your church. In this chapter, I've mentioned four categories of potential lay people: young Christians, women, the less likely, and those who need liberation. I'm not counseling you to immediately launch your lay people into small group ministry. All potential leaders will need training to enter small group ministry. We'll cover small group training in later chapters. I only want to broaden the scope of your vision for potential leaders in your church.

Young Christians

One of the most effective evangelists of the New Testament was the woman of Samaria — a new convert of a few hours. Immediately after her encounter with God we read that the woman of Samaria went into action:

> "[She] . . . went back to the town and said to the people, Come, see a man who told me everything I ever did. Could this be the Christ?' They came out of the town and made their way toward him . . . Many of the Samaritans from that town believed in him because of the woman's testimony, 'He told me everything I ever did.' So when the Samaritans came to him, they urged him to stay with them, and he stayed two days. And because of his words many more became believers. They said to the woman, 'We no longer believe just because of what you said; now we have heard for ourselves, and we know that this man really is the Savior of the world.' (Jn. 4:28-30, 40-42).

How long did it take the Samaritan woman to get into ministry? Long enough to go into the village and come back! Don't miss the opportunity of using newer Christians in cell leadership. Jesus didn't nor did Paul.

Fatima, a newly baptized Christian, planted the first daughter cell from my own small group in Quito, Ecuador. Plagued with a debilitating bone disease, she felt compelled to share the gospel while there was still time. With the zeal that characterized the Samaritan woman, Fatima gathered her non-Christian family and friends for the first meeting. Her house was packed — some had arrived two hours early. They listened to the gospel message with rapt attention and, in the months that followed, several of them decided to follow Jesus Christ. Fatima's zeal and effectiveness clarified to me the importance of using newer Christians in small group ministry.

Peter Wagner reminds us that the potential for evangelism is much higher with new Christians than with mature ones.[2] This is primarily due to the fact that new Christians still have contacts with non-Christians. New Christians are enthusiastic. When they are not allowed to evangelize or serve right away, they become stagnant and lose their enthusiasm. Our problem so often is not seeing far enough down the road. We fail to connect the person who walks down the aisle to receive Jesus with future leadership in cell ministry. For lack of proper guidance, many potential cell leaders slide out the back door.

WOMEN

When I visited Yoido Full Gospel Church in 1997, I desired to know how this church succeeds in raising up so many cell leaders. One clear answer is that Cho trusts his lay people. He believes in the priesthood of all believers — whether they are men or women.

Today, David Cho's church is the prime example of a cell ministry that was launched by women and that uses women as the vast majority of cell leaders.[3] For years, Cho tried doing everything himself. One night he tried to baptize 300 people, and he had a physical breakdown that required ten years to overcome. His doctor prescribed strict bed rest. In desperation, he asked his board of elders to help him pastor the church. They refused — even considered finding another pastor.[4] With few alternatives, he gathered all the women leadership in his church, saying, "I need you to help me to pastor this church." They said, "Yes, pastor, we'll help you. They began to pastor and care for the church through the cell ministry. When Cho had his physical breakdown, there were some 3,000 people in his church. When he finally recovered in 1978, there were 15,000 people in his church.

In Cho's church today over 19,000 of the 25,000 cell groups are led by women.[5] The women who lead cell groups in Cho's church are not considered authoritative Bible teachers. Rather, their authority is derived from their submission to Pastor Cho's leadership. These women leaders are seen as facilitators ministering under Pastor Cho. Their job is to encourage the spiritual life of the group by visiting, praying, and ministering to each member. New Hope Community Church in Portland, Oregon views their women leaders in the same way. At NHCC an equal number of men and women are Lay Pastors.[6]

Most of the rapidly growing cell churches make extensive use of women in ministry. This is not a new phenomenon. Back in the days when Wesley turned England upside down through a powerful small-group ministry, the majority of his cell leaders were women.[7] The proliferation of cell groups creates a need for more leaders and it becomes especially critical that a church not eliminate 50 percent of its potential small-group leaders on the basis of gender.

THE LESS LIKELY

John Wesley mastered the art of using every possible leader. Commenting on his genius, Howard Snyder says:

> One hears today that it is hard to find enough leaders for small groups or for those to carry on the other responsibilities of the church. Wesley put one in ten, perhaps one in five, to work in significant ministry and leadership. And who were these people? Not the educated or the wealthy with time on their hands, but laboring men and women, husbands and wives and young folks with little or no training, but with spiritual gifts and eagerness to serve . . . Not only did Wesley reach the masses; he made leaders of thousands of them.[8]

My survey of over 700 cell leaders in eight distinct cultures confirms Wesley's strategy. I discovered that the potential to lead a growing, successful cell group does not reside with the gifted, the educated, or those with vibrant personalities. The answer, rather, is hard work. I discovered that male and female, educated and uneducated, married and single, shy and outgoing, those gifted as teachers and those gifted as evangelists, equally multiplied their small groups. The anointing for cell multiplication doesn't reside with a mysterious few.

THOSE WHO ARE BOUND-UP

Most of us would have passed over Mary Magdalene because of her sad spiritual state (possessed by seven demons). Yet Jesus released her and used her mightily. According to the gospel writers, after his resurrection, Jesus appeared first to Mary Magdalene (Mark 16:9).

Often the most effective cell leaders are God's treasures that simply need to be developed and unwrapped. Jesus is all-powerful. He's able to take the brokenness of sin, heal it, and transform us in the process.

I remember the first time I visited the International Charismatic Mission. I met a drug addict who had just come back from an Encounter Retreat. His eyes sparkled with the love of Jesus. He didn't know the Christian lingo and all the Christian culture habits, but he knew his mission. He had been touched with the flame of Jesus Christ. The International Charismatic Mission was ready to use this young man in the ministry. Yes, he had more training to complete before entering cell leadership. Yet it's through people like this young man that Bogota is being transformed by the gospel.

ANYONE CAN LEAD A CELL GROUP

The introverted, the uneducated, and those in the lower social bracket are just as successful in multiplying cell groups as their counterparts. Nor does one particular gift of the Spirit such as evangelism distinguish those who could multiply their groups from those who cannot. Successful cell leaders don't depend solely on their own gifts. They rely on the Holy Spirit as they marshal the entire cell to reach family, friends, and acquaintances.[9]

I encourage cell leaders to view all cell members as "potential cell leaders" and sponsor all of them to become cell leaders. I've noticed that there are far too many "assistant cell leaders" who do nothing but occupy a title. Such a title draped over one or two people often hinders other members from assuming the role of cell leader. Harold Weitsz, pastor of Little Falls Christian Centre in South Africa, echoes this thinking when he writes: "We do not speak of 'cell members' any longer, but of trainees to become cell leaders."[10] Granted, not everyone will lead a group for a variety of reasons. But as soon as a small-group system is infected with the thinking that only certain people can lead a group, many believers become frustrated, forever classified as incapable. As leaders, it's important to commit to training each believer to minister. We must commit ourselves 100% to the priesthood of all believers. I believe that we will reap a mighty harvest as we commit ourselves to prepare and use young Christians, women, the less likely, and everyone else in the congregation.

3

CELL REPRODUCTION:
THE GUIDING STAR OF LEADERSHIP DEVELOPMENT

Chuck Smith, the founder and senior pastor of Calvary Chapel, doesn't know who I am. Yet I consider Chuck Smith to be my pastor. As a brand new believer in Christ, I grew spiritually under Pastor Chuck's teaching. As I attended Calvary Chapel, I noticed many new faces on Pastor Chuck's pastoral team. Chuck wasn't satisfied by holding tightly to his pastors. He allowed them to enter the pastoral team for a season, but the goal was to send them out to start their own churches. Some of the largest churches in the world today, like Harvest Christian Fellowship (Pastor Greg Laurie), are led by former members of Chuck Smith's pastoral team. Because Pastor Chuck sent them into the harvest, he constantly needed new pastors to take their place.

Many small groups fail to develop new leadership because of an inward focus. The same leader and members stay together for years and eventually stagnate. Healthy small groups are constantly in need of new leaders because they seek to expand the kingdom and reproduce new groups.

BIBLICAL EXAMPLES OF REPRODUCTION

The church will only expand its influence in the world by reproducing its most powerful unit, the cell group. Therefore, just as a family guarantees its legacy by producing children, so must a cell group seek to reproduce life in others by producing new groups.

God's desire for reproduction is seen in the first chapter of Genesis: "God blessed mankind saying, 'Be fruitful and increase in number; fill the earth and subdue it. Rule over the fish of the sea and the birds of the air and over every living creature that moves on the ground'" (Gen. 1:28).

In a similar fashion, God blessed Abraham at the age of 99 saying, "I will confirm my covenant between me and you and will greatly increase your numbers" (Gen. 17:2). Jesus commands the same type of fruitfulness in John 15:8: "This is to my Father's glory, that you bear much fruit, showing yourselves to be my disciples." At the end of His ministry, Jesus said to His disciples: "All authority in heaven and on earth has been given to me. Therefore go and make disciples of all nations, baptizing them in the name of the Father and of the Son and of the Holy Spirit" (Mt. 28:18-19). The only viable way to reap the harvest is through the reproduction of cell groups, and this demands more leaders.[1]

MAKE YOUR SMALL GROUPS OUTREACH ORIENTED

Our natural human tendency steers us to maintain the normal, the status quo. We want the warmth and communion of the small group to continue forever. It won't. Like Chuck Smith learned, through giving one receives. In refreshing others, we are refreshed. Members of a team will never reach full potential unless they are allowed to grow to the point of leading others. Unless provision is made for a cell member to become a cell leader, he never has the chance to exercise his spiritual muscles and truly depend on the living God.

Recently, I received a compliment from one of my cell leaders. He said, "Joel, the reason I like this church is because you were concerned about me. You kept on inviting me to your cell group. But you didn't stop there. You prepared me and launched me out into ministry." Paul is fulfilled in his new cell leadership position. I could have held tightly to Paul in my own cell group. But by sending him out, he's able to exercise his own gifts and talents while the church continues to grow.

It's my growing conviction that cell reproduction is the chief motivation behind leadership development. Effective cell churches tailor their training to fulfill the objective of cell multiplication. The genetic code of cell multiplication is instilled in each leader from the first moment he or she begins leading the new group.

Cell multiplication is so central to cell ministry that the goal of cell leadership is not fulfilled until the new groups are also reproducing. A new group can only be considered viable if it eventually births a new group itself.

REPRODUCTION GUIDES OTHER LEADERSHIP DISCIPLINES

The theme of reproduction must guide cell ministry. The desired end is that each cell grows and multiplies. When you are crystal clear on this point, leadership training becomes focused. I didn't always believe in cell reproduction as the guiding star of cell ministry. In my first cell manual (1992) I wrote, "The focus of the cells is evangelism and discipleship." On the same page I also said, "The principal objective of our system is that the members of each cell experience true fellowship with each other." At that time, I didn't try to connect evangelism, discipleship, and fellowship. As I look back, I readily admit that I was confused about the central focus of cell ministry. I had read some articles and books, and afterwards tried to pull it all together. Maybe you've done the same thing.

Try to grasp the bigger picture that cell reproduction draws. To multiply a group, a leader must pray daily for cell members, prepare himself spiritually before God, visit the members regularly, make numerous phone calls to invite newcomers, prepare the cell lesson, make any other arrangements, and above all, train new leadership to lead the new cells. It's a total package. If the cell leader only focuses on evangelism, many will slip out the back door. If he only centers his attention on discipleship, the group will grow inward and probably stagnate. If the leader concentrates solely on small group dynamics, leadership development will suffer. Effective cell leaders possess a clear aim for the group and gently lead the group to fulfill the goal of multiplication.

The cell leader should delegate responsibility as much as possible. He must stimulate others in the group to visit, make phone calls, and participate in the cell. The cell leader simply makes sure these disciplines take place.

REPRODUCTION FOCUSES CELL LEADER TRAINING

If cell reproduction is the principal goal of each cell leader, then leadership training must fulfill that purpose. This focus will dispose of fuzziness and fog from the first day of training. It will hone the leader in those areas that will make cell multiplication a reality. It will transform generalized training programs into specialized training. Instead of training a standing army, it will prepare a lightning task force that concentrates on the most important task of cell leadership.

A clear focus on cell reproduction will help potential leadership gain confidence and clarity. It will also help the leader to pastor the members and train new ones. Why? So that the group will reproduce itself.

REPRODUCTION DEFINES LEADERSHIP DEVELOPMENT

A number of cell disciplines contribute to cell multiplication, but I believe the primary one is leadership development. Successful cell churches understand that without new leadership, multiplication will not happen. The principal job of the cell leader is to train the next cell leader — not to fill the house with guests. Your primary objective in small group ministry is not to build groups. Rather, we develop small groups so we can build leaders, because leaders build groups. Remember, a small group is never an end in itself. Empowering and releasing people to lead is the goal. Non-Christians must be converted into members and then developed into leaders. George says, "But small groups are not the solution to what the church needs most desperately. Rather, churches rise and fall on the availability of trained, talented, and Spirit-gifted leadership. And the best possible context anyone has ever discovered for developing leadership occurs because of a small group."[2]

4

DEVELOPING
BIBLICAL LEADERS

Demosthenes, the greatest orator of the ancient world, stuttered! The first time he tried to make a public speech, he was laughed off the rostrum. Julius Caesar was an epileptic; Beethoven was deaf, as was Thomas Edison. Charles Dickens was lame; so was Handel. Homer was blind; Plato was a hunchback; Sir Walter Scott was paralyzed. Each of these leaders was willing to press onward, in spite of their weaknesses.[1]

It's hard to classify exactly what a leader should look like. Herb Miller, in his excellent book, *The Empowered Leader*, said, "But I am convinced that great leaders are rarely normal, well-adjusted people. Frankly, which of us is not a bit tired of normalcy anyway?"[2]

Here is a great icebreaker to use among cell leaders: What kind of characteristics should the perfect leader possess? Don't worry too much if you get as many answers as those attending your group.[3] It's difficult, if not impossible, to find an exact definition of leadership.

The study of leadership is broad and varied. The numerous definitions of leadership provide validity to this quote by Bennis and Nanus: ". . . leadership is the most studied and least understood topic of any in the social sciences. . . . Leadership is like the Abominable Snowman, whose footprints are everywhere but who is nowhere to be seen."[4] These experts in the field of leadership go on to say:

> Literally thousands of empirical investigations of leaders have been conducted in the last seventy-five years alone, but no clear and unequivocal understanding exists as to what distinguishes leaders from non-leaders, and perhaps more important, what distinguishes effective leaders from ineffective leaders and effective organizations from ineffective organizations.[5]

If you're contemplating future leadership, be encouraged. God uses all kinds of leaders. There is no such thing as the perfect leader. Nor is there one mold labeled leadership. God wants to use you in your uniqueness. Leadership has many personalities. Although the Bible doesn't promote one "personality type" for great leadership, it does give us the characteristics of effective leadership. The following provides clues to biblical leadership.

OLD TESTAMENT PRINCIPLES

When I do cell training, I know that I need to share the following leadership requirements because God requires them. Several of these traits can be summarized in one phrase: dependence upon God. God is looking for leaders who have the right heart attitude. The following biblical references actually mention what God expects of a leader:

Exodus 18:25:
- ☑ Virtuous
- ☑ Delegates responsibility

Deuteronomy 17:15-20
- ☑ Elected by God (v.15)
- ☑ Committed believer (15)
- ☑ Dependent on God (16-17)
- ☑ An obedient student of the Bible (18,19)
- ☑ Manifests humility (v. 20)

I Samuel 16:7
- ☑ Has a heart dedicated to God

II Samuel 23:3 & Leviticus 25:43-53
- ☑ Demonstrates reverence for God

DEPENDENCE ON GOD

A godly Christian leader must desire God above all else. This quality of hungering and thirsting for God will guide the other skills. Jesus says to seek first His kingdom and His righteousness, and all these things will be given to you (Mt. 6:33). The strongest disciples are those who long for the presence of God. The Holy Spirit will be hindered if a leader is spiritually indifferent. A person who is not allowing the Holy Spirit to work in his or her own life can hardly be a channel for His working in the group. The Holy Spirit is the great Leader, so we need him in our ministry to be effective. His will and glory above all else. "My food," said Christ, "is to do the will of my Father and to finish His work" (John 4:34).

Spirituality is a prerequisite for effective cell leaders. I'm not referring here to a super-spirituality, which characterizes certain high-minded people. We are all aware of those who use their "spirituality" to mask deep-seated pride. Rather, I'm talking about a humble dependence on God. I'm referring to a person who truly believes "that apart from Him, we can do nothing."

Ray Prior, the president of the Borden Corporation, one of the largest business structures in America, was asked how he led such a large corporation. He answered, "Each morning when I wake up, I meet with the Lord and begin to listen to His voice. In that period of time, I ask Him to bring to my mind the needs of the key men who report directly to me. As I think about their weaknesses, I plan my day."[6] Let's follow the example of Ray Prior, staying in tune with Jesus Christ moment by moment.

Jesus tells us that the Father is looking for such worshipers (John 4:24). Effective leaders understand that the most important preparation for the leader before the cell meeting begins is to wait in His presence. As the leader waits before God, he or she will receive direct orders from God. Lesson preparation is important, but spiritual preparation comes first. More important than time spent pouring over the cell lesson is quality time with God. I agree with Icenogle when he says, "The hope for healthy Christian small groups lies in group leaders who 'are willing to be led' by the Spirit."[7] Cell leaders must lead the group in the power of the Holy Spirit.

OVERCOMING OBSTACLES

Anyone studying leadership in the Old Testament is obliged to take note of the life of Nehemiah. Notice some key principles from Nehemiah's life:

☑ Passion for the glory of God (1:4)

☑ Dynamic life of prayer (1:5-11)

☑ Willingness to fulfill his own prayer (1:11; 4:8,9)

☑ Sacrificial life (2:1-7)

☑ Wise plans (2:4-7)

☑ Contagious vision (2:17, 18 & 4:1-14)

☑ Just life (5:1-13)

☑ Ministry of teaching (8:9, 18)

☑ Hatred of sin (13:25)

Nehemiah possessed God's passion, was willing to get involved, knew where to go, how to get it done, and was able to motivate people toward the fulfillment of his goal. His leadership transformed a depressed and oppressed group of God's people into a lightning task force, capable of accomplishing God's purpose.

Yet, if I could pinpoint the most important trait from the life of Nehemiah, it would be the ability to overcome obstacles. Trials and tribulations piled up against Nehemiah — to the point of trouncing him. Yet, we read how he overcame them time and time again. He was so consumed by his God-given task and vision that he never allowed obstacles and difficulties to deter him.

Martin Luther King Jr. once said, "The ultimate measure of a man is not where he stands in moments of comfort and convenience, but where he stands at times of challenge and controversy." Nehemiah lived in the midst of adversity but he faced it, confronted it, and triumphed over it. Cell leadership can learn from his example.

Miriam Richards is the leader of a young professional's group. As a single mother, she has many personal obstacles to overcome — long work days and endless motherly responsibilities. Yet, she doesn't allow these very real obstacles to stop her from effective cell leadership. She sees them as stepping-stones. "Cell leadership has done wonders for me," she told us during one leadership meeting. "Each week, I'm forced to depend upon God as I prepare. I'm dependent on Him to help me find solutions to the needs of my group." Miriam leads a solid, growing group, in which two atheists regularly attend.

I've noticed that some cell leaders always have an excuse. You know what pastor, "No one in my neighborhood is open to the gospel." "This cell ministry is hard, I just don't have the time."

Ten spies came back with a report based on the *reality* of the situation. "There are giants in the land! There is no way we can win this war." Joshua and Caleb saw two realities: the giants and the God who made them. They came back excited for the chance to see God's mighty power at work. "Let's go for it. Right now. This land is full of milk and honey and we serve a big God. He's easily able to take us into the land and bring us the victory. Let's go."

Do you see obstacle or opportunity? Herb Miller gives this advice to leaders, "Never sidestep challenges. Grab every charging bull by the horns and slap him twice across the face. Remind him that God is in charge of you . . ." [8]

A cell leader will face moments of discouragement, loneliness, and pain. Conflicts often surface in a cell group due to personality differences, constant talkers, overly "spiritual ones," late arrivers, poor communication, and cultural differences. A cell leader might even face direct criticism from members of the group. A common assumption that many cell leaders make is that all conflict is "bad" and should be avoided if possible. Yet, if conflict can lead to deeper consideration of the issues at hand, and if it challenges members to look at their own behaviors, then it's beneficial to the group.

Nehemiah overcame the obstacles, but he also had his moments of intense discouragement. Thomas Edison once remarked, "Many of life's failures are people who did not realize how close they were to success when they gave up." Edison tried 10,000 times before he finally found the right materials for the incandescent light bulb. Every time he failed he gained valuable information about what didn't work, bringing him closer to the solution.

New Testament Principles

Several New Testament passages specifically deal with leadership characteristics. I've summarized these traits in the following list. Notice how these characteristics focus on godliness and servanthood.

Mark 10:42-45
- ☑ Domination is the world's leadership style
- ☑ Servant hood is the leadership style of the disciple
- ☑ Service through the cell ministry

Acts 6:3
- ☑ A good testimony
- ☑ Filled with the Spirit
- ☑ Filled with wisdom

Romans 12:8
- ☑ Diligence

Timothy 3:1-13 (Titus 1: 5-10)
- ☑ Social qualities
  - A pure life (3:2,3)
  - A good reputation (3:7)
- ☑ Moral qualities
  - Husband of one wife (3:2)
  - Not given to wine (3:3)

☑ Mental qualities
- Respectable (3:2)
- Self-controlled (3:2)
- Able to teach (3:2)

☑ Personal qualities
- Gentle (3:3)
- Hospitable (3:2)
- Not a lover of money (3:3)

☑ Domestic qualities
- House in order (3:2,4,5)

GODLY CHARACTER

D.L. Moody once commented, "Character is what you are in the dark."[9] Most of the requirements in the New Testament involve character. Virtues such as honesty, faithfulness, and good judgment are synonymous with New Testament leadership. No amount of talent or giftedness can replace these characteristics. Bad character qualities will ultimately disqualify a person from leadership.

As a young Christian studying at college in Long Beach, California, I witnessed to a friend in Biology class. She politely listened and even nodded, but nothing more. One evening several months later, I was eating with friends in a nearby restaurant. To my surprise, this girl from college appeared as our waitress for the evening. We talked, ordered our food, ate, and then asked for the bill. Trying to please us (at the expense of her boss), she came back saying, "I'm not going to write on the bill all of the food that you ate." God spoke to me immediately and I said to her, "I appreciate your gesture, but we're Christians and God wants us to pay for what we ate."

She was quite surprised and probably thought we were a bit weird, but the message was clear. Before leaving, I invited her to our church.

The next Sunday she showed up at church and said to me, "When you didn't accept my offer last week at the restaurant, I knew that you were a Christian." This girl had heard me talk about Jesus previously at college, but she had to see Jesus played out in my character before believing. My actions, as opposed to my words, made the difference in her life.

People are watching our lives. They want to make sure that our actions correspond with our words before receiving the gospel message. They want to make sure that the leader they are going to follow is credible and honest. Godly character refers to Christ's work in our actions, attitude, and daily Christian living.

Today we face a dearth of godly character. We're inclined to cry out with the Psalmist, "Help, LORD, for the godly are no more" (Psalm 12:1). So many gifted Christians, who minister to multitudes, fall prey to their own moral weaknesses.

The words of Paul to Timothy are pertinent for this issue of character, "Don't let anyone look down on you because you are young, but set an example for the believers in speech, in life, in love, in faith and in purity" (1 Tim. 4:12). Paul knew that Timothy was surrounded by older critics who wanted nothing more than to see him fall. Ephesus, though one of the most prominent cities in the Roman world, was filled with idolatry, orgies, and magic. It was in Ephesus that "A number who had practiced sorcery brought their scrolls together and burned them publicly. When they calculated the value of the scrolls, the total came to fifty thousand drachmas" (Acts 19:19).

Paul's advice to Timothy in the midst of temptation and corruption was, in effect, "silence your critics by your actions." Be an example to the believers . . . in purity. The word purity (hagnos) is always used with a moral sense. It is not limited to sins of the flesh, but covers purity in motive as well as in acts. The age-old saying rings true: "Actions speak louder than words." Cell leaders must maintain godly ethics and character at all times.

Where I'm currently ministering, people often say: "In Ecuador lots of oil flows." The oil is the oil of bribery, not petroleum. The system in Ecuador flows smoothly when it's greased with lots of bribes.

Daniel Santana was one of my most trusted cell leaders. This man was respected as a first class architect, but more importantly as a godly Christian leader. Daniel confessed to me that by refusing to offer bribes, he lost many contracts as an architect. Because of his refusal to mess around with sin, he maintained a pure testimony in the midst of a corrupt society. Make sure that what you are in the dark is the same person that lives in the day.

SERVANTHOOD

One characteristic of leadership that is unique to the New Testament is the concept of servanthood. Jesus taught His disciples to aspire to serve rather than "lord over." According to Jesus, the greatest leaders were the most diligent servants. He uses Himself as an illustration: "For even the Son of Man did not come to be served, but to serve, and to give his life as a ransom for many" (Mt. 10:42-45).

Jesus continually modeled this attitude with His small group to the point of washing their feet (John 13). Cell leaders must be willing to extend themselves as servants to the entire group. Steve Barker points out:

> . . . a cell group requires lots of service. When a group starts, someone must decide on the who, when, where, why and how. This translates into placing phone calls, reserving rooms, arranging chairs, making coffee, offering rides, reminding people and finally, making introductions. Such nitty-gritty work is thankless but necessary. It's the behind-the-scenes effort

that often determines whether the initial small group meeting is a miserable failure or a promising beginning.[10]

Although it's always good to delegate, ultimately the cell leader is responsible for the activities in the group, the order of the meeting, where the group will meet, the refreshments, follow-up on the newcomers. A servant's heart is a necessary ingredient in effective cell ministry.

LEADERSHIP REQUIREMENTS IN CELL CHURCHES

The Bible gives clear guidelines for Christian leadership, but they are only guidelines. The specific application of biblical leadership principles varies from church to church. How long, for example, should a person know Jesus before leading a cell group? Paul says in 1 Timothy 3:6 that a bishop must not be ". . . a recent convert, or he may become conceited and fall under the same judgment as the devil." But what does the word "recent" mean? The Greek the word "recent" literally means "newly-planted," but we still need more information for a precise application. Does a "recent convert" mean three weeks or three years? We also must remember that Paul was referring to the office of bishop, the highest office in the church. Is it correct to place the requirements of bishop on a cell leader today?

In eight of the world's largest cell churches, the length of time a potential leader needs to be converted varied from three months to three years.[11] The average length of knowing Jesus before leading a cell group was one year. It must be noted, however, that the International Charismatic Mission, which is the fastest growing cell church today, turns unbelievers into cell leaders in six months. These new believers still have fresh contact with their non-Christian *oikos* relationships and often become evangelists.

Although the requirements vary from church to church, the core requirements of salvation, membership, water baptism, cell attendance, and completion of specific cell training applied in all the churches. The amount and content of the training, however, varies greatly from church to church (if you are interested in more information on this subject, see Appendix B).

BIBLICAL VALUES

We've looked at core characteristics of biblical leaders, which all leaders must emulate. These characteristics must form and transform the convictions and lifestyle of cell leadership. While clinging to the overarching set of biblical values and characteristics mentioned previously, effective cell leaders manifest certain leadership and ministry values that are especially helpful in small group ministry.

The dictionary defines a value as "principle, standard, or quality considered worthwhile or desirable."[12] Synonyms for value include excellence, worth, merit, priority, and superiority.[13] Values are priorities that grip us so completely that we practice them. Head values are what we share when asked to describe to others what's important to us. Heart values are those seen after we look back on our time usage over an average week. Head values reflect great intentions while heart values are a stark view of what really makes us tick. In other words, we value what we do and we do what we value. If you want to know what someone values, notice where he spends the majority of his time. Chapters five and six highlight the values essential to good cell leadership.

The Values of Effective

Cell Leaders

Eight months after we started the Republic Church, I spoke to a cell group that was meeting about a half hour from the church. The group was very discouraged and even doubted whether or not they should continue. I spoke to them about the effectiveness of the cell strategy and how God wanted to use them to be a shining light in their own neighborhood.

One housewife who attended that meeting was Lorgia Haro. Her husband was a non-Christian. She seemed to possess no extraordinary talents and was actually a very shy person. Yet, Lorgia was willing to step out in her weakness and trust God for the impossible.

I then went home to the U.S. for two years. When I returned to the Republic Church in 1997, I discovered that more than 30 new people were attending the celebration services at the Republic Church due to the ministry of Lorgia Haro. Most of those 30 people were saved under her ministry and seven were baptized in our church. Now there are over 70 people attending the church as a result of her ministry, 12 baptized, and she has multiplied her cell group seven times. What values do people like Lorgia embrace that make them effective?

WILLINGNESS TO RISK

A missionary organization wanted to send helpers to Dr. Livingstone in Africa. The mission leader wrote, "Have you found a good road to where you are? If so, we want to send other men to join you." Livingstone replied, "If you have men who will come only if they know there is a good road, I don't want them. I want men who will come even if there is no road at all." Leaders make their own roads; they blaze their own trails. They are willing to risk for Jesus Christ. In *The Leadership Challenge*, authors James Kouzes and Barry Posner say, "Leaders venture out. Those who lead others to greatness seek and accept challenge. Leaders are pioneers — people who are willing to step out into the unknown. They're willing to take risks, to innovate and experiment in order to find new and better ways of doing things."[1]

Effective leaders are open to ideas. They are willing to try untested approaches and to accept the risks that accompany all experiments. Successful leaders learn from their failures and become stronger as a result. For the successful leader, failure is the springboard of hope. Jesus understood this principle. He allowed His disciples to experience ministry and even fail. But when they failed, Jesus used the experience of failure to train them more specifically.

We all make mistakes. Think of the Munich schoolmaster who told a ten-year old Albert Einstein, "You'll never amount to very much." Or consider the Decca record company executive who in 1962 refused to give an upstart British rock group a contract. "We don't like the Beatles' sound," he explained. "Groups with guitars are on their way out."[2]

Don't fear mistakes. As Elbert Hubbard said, "The greatest mistake one can make in life is to be continually fearing you will make one." We can learn from our mistakes. Granted, they hurt, but you won't learn unless you make them. A young man, eager to climb into the driver's seat of his organization, went into the old man's office and said, "Sir, as you know, I've been appointed by the board to succeed you as president of the bank, and I'd be very grateful for any counsel and help that you could give to me."

The old man said, "Son, sit down. I have two words of counsel for you. Two words." "What are they?" asked the young executive. "Right Decisions," said the boss. The young man thought a moment and said, "Sir, that's very helpful, but how does one go about making those right decisions?" The old man responded, "One word: Experience." "Thank you, sir," said the young man. "I'm sure that will be helpful. But really sir, how does one go about gaining experience?" The old man smiled and said, "Two words: Wrong Decisions."[3]

Did you know?

☑ Babe Ruth struck out 1,330 times. In between his strikeouts, he hit 714 home runs.

☑ Abraham Lincoln failed twice as a business person and was defeated in six state and national elections before being elected president of the United States.

☑ R. H. Macey failed in retailing seven times before his store in New York became a success.

☑ Louisa May Alcott's family encouraged her to find work as a servant or seamstress rather than write. She wrote, and *Little Women* is still popular more than 125 years later.

☑ Theodor S. (Dr. Seuss) Geisel's first children's book was rejected by 23 publishers. The twenty-fourth publisher sold six million copies.[4]

Teddy Roosevelt asserted, "He who makes no mistakes, makes no progress." As a leader, you'll make plenty of mistakes. Just remember that mistakes are helpers, not hindrances. Leaders should expect mistakes and thank the Lord for them. They help chart the course with necessary adjustments that will keep small groups on the road. When mistakes are made, quickly admit them, learn from them, and move ahead.

In an article in *Slate Magazine* about the success of the Silicon Valley, Michael Lewis wrote:

> . . . the Valley has responded by making failure something of a badge of honor. An entrepreneur who has gone broke three times in a row can, if he has a fourth good idea, find people who will back him. Some of his financial backers will put up their money because he has gone broke three times in a row. "If I am given a choice between a guy who has failed a couple of times and a guy who is starting his first," says the Valley's ruling venture capitalist, John Doerr of Kleiner Perkins Caufield & Byers, "I will fund the guy who has failed."[5]

Do you see failure as a badge of honor in your ministry, or a curse to be avoided at all costs? Embrace failure and allow it to work for you. Don't be afraid of it.

Walking on the water toward His disciples, Jesus said, "Take courage! It is I. Don't be afraid." "Lord, if it's you," Peter replied, "tell me to come to you on the water." "Come," he said. Then Peter got down out of the boat, walked on the water and came toward Jesus. But when he saw the wind, he was afraid and, beginning to sink, cried out, "Lord, save me!" Immediately Jesus reached out his hand and caught him. "You of little faith," he said, "why did you doubt?" (Mt.14:27-32).

Never belittle Peter for his doubt — at least he was willing to try. I admire someone more if he has tried and failed than someone who sits in the boat, warm and content. Just two chapters later, Peter jumps into the fray and is the first to confirm Christ's Deity, "You are the Christ, the Son of the living God" (Mt. 16:16). Jesus blessed Peter for his reply. Shortly thereafter, with fresh confidence, Peter begins to rebuke Jesus and the Lord says, "Get behind me, Satan! You are a stumbling block to me; you do not have in mind the things of God, but the things of men." Granted, Peter made his share of mistakes. But his willingness to try, and even fail, supplied him with insight that few of the other apostles possessed.

I admire cell leaders who are willing to walk on water. These are the risk takers, the rock climbers of cell ministry. I've had the privilege of meeting some of them in my ministry and travels, and I pray constantly that God would provide more of their kind. Don't be afraid to launch out into the deep. Jesus will welcome you and sustain you.

DILIGENCE

There is an old saying: "Champions don't become champions in the ring — they are merely recognized there." The diligent, secret training before the fight begins propels a boxer to win. Successful leaders work hard and success naturally follows. Scripture clearly teaches that diligence precedes success.

Those leaders who are willing to work hard — willing to "do their best" — multiply their cells. The Scripture teaches that the desires of the diligent are fully satisfied. God uses those who diligently seek Him and labor for His glory. The Bible is full of Scriptures that talk about diligence. The Greek word for diligence (*spoudé*) means:

☑ Quick movement in the interests of a person or a cause
☑ To hasten oneself
☑ Speed in carrying out a matter

☑ Giving oneself trouble
☑ Active, industrious, zeal, effort, pains
☑ Standing in contrast to laziness

Let me give you an example of this word *spoudé* and how it is used in Scripture. In 2 Peter 3:12-14 the Scripture says: "So then, dear friends, since you are looking forward to this, *make every effort (spoudé)* to be found spotless, blameless and at peace with him." "Making every effort" is what diligence is all about.

Another well-known verse is Hebrews 4:10,11: "Let us, therefore, *make every effort (spoudé)* to enter that rest, so that no one will fall by following their example of disobedience." God asked His people to make every effort to enter His chosen rest.

Most of us know and might have even memorized 2 Tim. 2:15: "*Do your best (spoudé)* to present yourself to God as one approved, a workman who does not need to be ashamed and who correctly handles the word of truth." God calls His people to do their best.

John Wesley is a perfect example of this diligence. Wesley forced himself out of bed by four o'clock every morning, and seldom slept later than five. By slavishly keeping his daily diary, he bound himself to a careful accounting of his time so that he would not waste a moment. Wesley's achievements:

☑ From the age of 36 onwards, he traveled 225,000 miles on horseback
☑ He preached over 40,000 sermons — approximately 3 each day!
☑ He left behind a church of 100,000 members and 10,000 cell groups

God used Wesley, but Wesley was also willing to be used by God. He was willing to be that vessel through which God could work.

Wesley gave himself completely to God's work and God manifested His mighty power through him.

INSPIRATION VERSUS PERSPIRATION

Thomas Edison once said that genius is 99% perspiration and 1% inspiration. He proved this by his life. Are you willing to press on in spite of the failures in your life? Conrad Hilton, the famous hotel executive, once said, "Success seems to be connected with action. Successful people keep moving. They make mistakes, but they don't quit."

Basketball legend Larry Bird excelled at shooting free throws by practicing five hundred shots each morning before school. Demosthenes of ancient Greece became the greatest orator by reciting verse with pebbles in his mouth and speaking over the roar of the waves at the seashore.[6]

Successful cell leaders keep on doing the things they know they should do. Through practice, their leadership is perfected. They are willing to do what it takes to make their cells successful.

JUST DO IT

Nike has set in motion a phrase that has caught fire throughout the world: JUST DO IT. Don't talk about it, just do it. Don't idealize it, just do it. Don't dream about it, just do it. Don't make excuses, just do it. This one phrase distinguishes effective leaders from those who endlessly spin their wheels and never go anywhere. The phrase "just do it" means that there is hard work ahead. Proverbs 14:23: "All hard work brings a profit, but mere talk leads only to poverty."

I found the following quote in one of the training manuals of the International Charismatic Mission (this church grew from 70 cells in

1991 to 20,000 cells today): "Often, while others are sleeping, the leader continues working, trying to find solutions for the problems of the group."[7] In other words, just do it! Go for it. Make it happen. Wake-up early; discover the problem and solve it. John Maxwell says, "Perhaps the most valuable result of all education is the ability to make yourself do the thing you have to do, when it ought to be done, whether you like it or not; it is the first lesson that ought to be learned."[8]

John Hancock Field's said, "All worthwhile men have good thoughts, good ideas, and good intentions, but precious few of them ever translate those into action."[9] This concept of translating intention into action is perhaps the most important leadership trait. Effective leaders do what they don't like to do. They force themselves to get the job done, to make that extra phone call, to pray daily for cell members and to take time for devotions. They not only dream dreams but they live dreams. They put feet to their prayers. NBA basketball star Jerry West once said, "You can't get too much done in life if you only work on the days when you feel good." Just do it, whether you feel like it or not.

THE ABILITY TO HANDLE CRITICISM

Criticism is especially tough for young leadership. No one likes a negative comment, and it's easy to personalize an otherwise general criticism. Most people tend to blame the leader when something goes wrong, even though it might have nothing to do with him or her. It's important that the leader doesn't receive criticism as a personal indictment. People tend to criticize without knowing all the facts. Only God knows every detail, so you can entrust the situation to Him. In 1 Corinthians 4:3-5, Paul says:

I care very little if I am judged by you or by any human court; indeed, I do not even judge myself. My conscience is clear, but that does not make me innocent. It is the Lord who judges me. Therefore judge nothing before the appointed time; wait till the Lord comes. He will bring to light what is hidden in darkness and will expose the motives of men's hearts. At that time each will receive his praise from God.

Ultimately the leader's success stands or falls before God. Paul declares, "We are not trying to please men but God, who tests our hearts. You know we never used flattery, nor did we put on a mask to cover up greed — God is our witness. We were not looking for praise from men, not from you or anyone else" (1 Th. 2:4-6).

When dealing with criticism, keep in mind these three principles:

First, see the painful experience as an opportunity to grow in your faith. Remember that the apostle Paul gloried in his weakness and delighted in insults, hardships, and persecutions (1 Corinthians 11:9b, 10).

Second, be as honest and up-front as possible. Don't avoid conflict. Talk with the person. Conflict grows through secrecy but fades with openness and truth.

Bill Gates believes that a large part of his success at Microsoft has to do with confronting bad news and not hiding from it. He says, "I think the most important job, as a CEO is to listen for bad news. If you don't act on it, your people will eventually stop bringing bad news to your attention. And that's the beginning of the end."[10]

Third, don't be afraid to apologize as a leader — even before the whole group. The Bible warns about covering up our sin (Proverbs 28:13). The apostle John said,

If we claim to be without sin, we deceive ourselves and the truth is not in us. If we confess our sins, he is faithful and just

and will forgive us our sins and purify us from all
unrighteousness. If we claim we have not sinned, we make
him out to be a liar and his word has no place in our lives
(1 John 1:8-10).

Leaders must admit their failure before God and the group. By so
doing, a leader will receive more respect from the group and the group
itself will become more transparent.

GOAL ORIENTATION

Donald McGavran, the father of the church growth movement, states,
"Nothing focuses effort like setting a goal."[11] It's essential that each cell
leader set clear goals for the group. Those who set specific goals
multiply their groups more rapidly than those who do not. Effective
goal setting is the primary catalyst behind successful cell
multiplication.

Many leaders refuse to make goals and thus accept whatever
happens — often very little. Those leaders who don't set goals may be
working just as hard as their counterparts. Yet there is something
lacking. Their ministry is not going anywhere; it is seeking only to
maintain itself, rather than striving to become something better and
to reach even more persons with the gospel. Peter Wagner used to tell
his students, "The key is working smart, not just working hard."[12]
Setting specific, visible goals will focus the work of a cell leader and
make his or her dreams attainable. Nevertheless, many people don't
know how to set goals. Here are some guidelines:

First, a cell leader must set deadlines for his goals. When will the
project be completed? Most leaders find that they are more productive
when they have deadlines. A great goal has a starting point and an
ending point.

The specific goal in Cho's church is for each cell group to win one family to Christ every six months. To keep his cell leaders focused on that goal, Cho writes, "I pressure them, motivate them, and remind them constantly."[13] If the group does not accomplish that goal, Cho sends them to Prayer Mountain for an extended period of prayer.[14] At the International Charismatic Mission the young professional group made this goal:[15]

☑ Bring two new people to the group each week.
☑ Multiply the cell group every three months.

Your specific goal will undoubtedly be different because of your context and purpose. The main point is clarity. Fuzzy goals go nowhere while specific goals provide rails for your faith, prayers, and actions.

Second, make sure the goal is attainable. A leader might think that a huge goal will demonstrate his faith in God, so he launches a goal that flies in the face of reality. No one backs the goal because it's unattainable. Ian MacGregor, former AMAX Corporation chairman of the board said, "I work on the same principle as people who train horses. You start with low fences, easily achieved goals, and work up. It's important in management never to ask people to try to accomplish goals they can't accept." Make sure your goals are achievable.

Third, make the goals visible.[16] You can post them in your office, bedroom, or car — anyplace where you will see them every day. One cell church I visited posted goals for the upcoming year in the cell offices, the church sanctuary, and even in the reception area. Needless to say, the church is continually reminded of them.

VISIONARY LEADERSHIP

Vision is the mother of goal setting. The two are intimately related. Goals are incubated in a warm, visionary environment. The environment that I'm referring to is prayer and meditation. Vision, therefore, is primarily a Divine initiative — a gift from God. Vision doesn't spring from our own human whims and emotions; rather, God communicates His vision to us and even gives us the grace to respond. William Beckham writes: "Vision is not something I catch but something that catches me. I do not act upon this vision, it acts upon me. . . . A vision is something working in our lives, not something we are working on."[17]

God told Abraham that he would be the father of many nations. Granted, Abraham experienced his doubts. But ultimately his testimony as recorded in the Word of God is that he held fast to God's vision:

> Against all hope, Abraham in hope believed and so became the father of many nations, just as it had been said to him, "So shall your offspring be." Without weakening in his faith, he faced the fact that his body was as good as dead — since he was about a hundred years old — and that Sarah's womb was also dead. Yet he did not waver through unbelief regarding the promise of God, but was strengthened in his faith and gave glory to God, being fully persuaded that God had power to do what he had promised (Rom. 4:18-21).

The vision captured Abraham, even in his weakened physical state. Abraham is our example of believing God's vision and acting on it.

If God is the one who imparts dreams and visions, we must remember that His dreams are often much larger than our own. In this way, He gets the glory when they are accomplished. He has the means to accomplish any dream that He initiates. His dreams are bigger than ours, and they call for us to expand the size of our mental playing field to accommodate His vision.

GET THE BLUEPRINT

Perhaps vision can be best described by the relationship between an architect and construction workers. Before the actual construction can begin, there must be a blueprint. This is the lesson that Stephen Covey would have us capture. He refers to vision as the first creation. Covey believes that it is the leader's primary task to nurture the first creation.[18] Others might put the vision into practice, but leaders birth the vision.

Tom Watson, the founder of IBM, attributed the phenomenal success of his company this way:

> I had a very clear picture of what the company would look like when it was finally done. You might say I had a model in my mind of what it would look like when the dream — my vision — was in place . . . Once I had that picture, I then asked myself how a company which looked like that would have to act. I then created a picture of how IBM would act when it was finally done . . . I then realized that, unless we began to act that way from the very beginning, we would never get there.[19]

To choose a direction, a leader must first have developed a mental image of a desirable future state for the cell or church. The critical point is that a vision articulates a view of a realistic, credible, attractive future, a condition that is better in some important ways than what currently exists. It is this distinction between the initial dream and the actual fulfillment that separates leaders from managers.

The leader spends his time with the first creation, the vision. He meditates on the vision, he broadens it, he clarifies it, he synthesizes it, and he communicates it. The manager, on the other hand, is like the construction worker who follows the blueprint, who manages the existing direction. By focusing attention on a vision, the leader guides the cell or church into a clear future.

I encourage cell leaders to dream about their cell group, to ask God to show them His desired direction for the group. I tell them to dream about those potential leaders who need to be developed, the multiplication of the group, and the spiritual growth of the cell members. Leaders should not spend their time doing the work of the ministry at the expense of spending time with Him. Jesus taught us that worship comes before service (Mt. 4:10; Lk. 10:38-42).

COMMUNICATE THE VISION

Rick Warren says, "The #1 task of leadership is to continually clarify and communicate the purpose of the organization."[20] In his seminars on the Purpose-Driven Church, he urges pastors to clearly communicate their vision through slogans, symbols, stories, and Scriptures.[21] After the vision has been clarified and made simple enough so that the followers can comprehend it, effective leaders use every opportunity to communicate it. Barna says, "Those leaders who have been most successful contend that you must take advantage of all opportunities, at all times, to share the vision."[22]

You can't talk too much about your vision. There is a subtle, self-condemning tendency to think that people are tired of hearing the vision. Don't believe it.[23] By continually casting the vision, you will instill in your people a clear sense of direction and eventually accomplish your goal.

ADJUST THE VISION

Vision should not be considered as only an esoteric, spiritual experience. Don't think that you can't make mid-stream corrections to your vision. Leaders often discover that their goals are not based in reality. They might have been so ideal, in fact, that the cell members became disinterested.[24] A vision that is not adjusted to reality will probably fizzle out. To avoid this, a vision should be monitored and tracked.[25] A vision must act as a compass in a stormy sea, and, like a compass, it will lose its value if it is not adjusted to take account of its surroundings.

Finally, dreaming or having a vision is never an end in itself. Successful leaders are able to translate the vision into reality. They are not content with merely dreaming; they must see their dreams turn into reality.

VISIONARY CELL CHURCH PASTORS

Visionary pastors lead the cell churches that I studied. The cell systems flowed from the vision of the Senior Pastors. Their ultimate church growth goals envisioned hundreds of thousands of people. They were out to conquer cities for Christ — not just grow churches. These pastors enjoyed immense authority because they excelled in capturing, articulating and implementing God-given dreams and visions. I detected a great respect and submission among the members of these churches because they knew that their pastors heard from God. Because of the pastoral vision, the congregations in turn sensed that they were part of a work greater than themselves.

The pastors of the largest cell churches in the world talk about the importance of dreaming big dreams. David Cho, for example, not only receives God's vision for his church, but he also teaches his under-shepherds to dream big dreams. Cho asks each cell leader to capture God's vision for his or her group, and then to write that vision down. Using those pieces of paper, he then asks the leaders to look at their visions and live them out.[26]

Senior Pastors must create the environment for rapid cell multiplication by constantly launching the vision. This primarily takes place in the ongoing training times, but it also should be heard in the announcements, the sermon, and the award ceremonies (in honor of cell groups that have given birth). Again, the goal of the top leadership is to instill this vision for cell multiplication into the thinking of the cell leaders. Ultimately, the cell leaders are the ground troops who make it happen.

6

THE PRIORITIES OF
EFFECTIVE CELL LEADERS

All cell leaders face the "tyranny of the urgent." With so many urgent issues facing the cell leader daily, which one will take priority? The needs are endless — fine-tuning the cell lesson, arranging for the refreshments, or providing transportation. Cell leaders find themselves overwhelmed with worship choruses, icebreakers, calls, and visits. While these tasks are noble, if the leader is not careful, they can draw him away from the most important duty — raising up new leaders.

Everything demands immediate attention, or does it? In the midst of the fast-paced life of a cell leader, are there any priorities? Do certain things demand more attention than others? Yes. The following are leadership priorities that effective cell leaders practice.

FOCUSED MENTORING

John Wesley once said, "Give me 100 men who hate nothing but sin and love God with all their hearts and I will shake the world for

Christ!" By the end of his life, John Wesley had converted a motley rag-tag group of believers into a mighty cell church army of 10,000 cells and 100,000 members.

Successful cell leaders look beyond the urgent present to future daughter cells and, due to that driving passion, they spend priority time training new leadership. This passion to raise up new leaders drives successful cell leaders to spend quality time with potential leadership. This passion converts common cell members into visionary new leaders. Successful cell leaders reflect John Maxwell's passion: "My goal is not to draw a following that results in a crowd. My goal is to develop leaders who become a movement."[1]

Sadly, this passion remains hidden in many cell leaders and churches. So often the leader focuses entirely on leading the small group and seeing it grow in number. The small group is king. All resources and training focus on life in the group — not training leaders for future groups. Small groups become an end in themselves.

True leadership success depends on your answer to this question: How many leaders have been spotted, trained, and deployed? Success in apprenticing future leaders is a biblical way of life. Moses tutored Joshua, and Elijah trained Elisha. The apostles were recruited and trained by Jesus. Barnabas discipled Paul who in turn developed Timothy. Cell leaders must develop the next leader at all costs.

In Matthew 28:18-20, Jesus sets forth clear marching orders for His young church. An analysis of these verses demonstrates that of the four principle verbs listed in Matthew 28:19-20 only the one "to make disciples" is used in a direct command form.[2] The three other verbs compliment the main task of disciple making. Christ's command is clear. We are called to guide each newcomer in the faith to full maturity.

Paul understood this discipling process well. He spent his whole life preparing others to carry on Christ's ministry. The passion for leadership development stirred Paul to advise his disciple Titus to stay in Crete so that, ". . . you might straighten out what was left unfinished and appoint elders in every town, as I directed you" (Titus 1:5). Christianity started in Crete but it wasn't established due to lack of leadership. Paul passed by the region earlier but could not complete the work at that time. Why? No leaders. So he asks Titus, his disciple, to finish the work by appointing godly leaders.

At the end of his life, he exhorted his own disciple, Timothy, "And the things you have heard me say in the presence of many witnesses entrust to reliable men who will also be qualified to teach others" (2 Timothy 2:2). Notice the reliability issue here. The work of passing the baton to successive generations of leadership must not stop due to a bad link in the chain. By all means, leadership development must continue. A cell leader's main task, therefore, should be to work his way out of a job by training cell members to lead the cell group. Far from losing a job, disciple-making leaders gain authority, new leadership, and cell multiplication. Concentration on leadership development helps a leader multiply his ministry over and over and over.

PRAYER

Effective leaders both prepare themselves through prayer as well as pray daily for those in the cell group. Effective cell leaders also go one step further and promote prayer within the cell group. "Cells are merely a conduit through which the Holy Spirit flows," we often tell our cell leaders. Cells quickly slip into "program mode" unless they are spiritually alive. Take, for example, the place of spiritual warfare in cell ministry. When cells start praying for their neighborhoods and cities, the demons tremble.

Prayer, like every other participatory event in the cell group, brings unity and encouragement to the cell members. In Acts 4, we read that group prayer brought unity and courage to the disciples. Cell prayer has the same power. Praying out loud can build relationships and community within the group.

I attended a cell meeting in which the leader asked the members to pick their favorite songs during the worship time. After each song the cell leader asked the person to explain why he or she picked that particular song. One lady, Theresa, picked a song about renewal, and later sobbed, "I had an angry confrontation with my ex-husband today." She blurted out, "I feel so dirty. Please pray for me." The responsive, Spirit-led cell leader immediately grabbed the nearest chair and asked the cell members to gather around her for prayer. Theresa felt cleansed and healed as she left that prayer time. She came to the meeting bruised and beaten down, but she left filled and encouraged.

The sensitive leader utilizes the style of prayer that best fits the context of the cell group. When non-Christians are present, for example, an "all-out fiery" prayer meeting is probably not the best. Silent prayer might be in order, or praying in pairs. Cell leaders must remain sensitive to the situation and utilize the type of prayer that best fits with the circumstances.

RADICAL EVANGELISM

After commitment to prayer, cell leaders must make it their goal to reach non-Christians.

In order to accomplish this goal, cell leaders should know the difference between cell evangelism and other types of evangelism. In a nutshell, cell evangelism is relational and ongoing as opposed to impersonal and immediate. Cell evangelism is a personal process of sharing the Good News about forgiveness of sin and new life in Jesus. Because of the personal, intimate atmosphere of small groups, evangelism happens naturally. Wuthnow, in his well-researched book,

Sharing the Journey, noted that small group evangelism in the United States is natural and authentic: "Group members do say they are sharing their faith, but they are not drawn to the formal programs of evangelism that many clergy advocate . . . They are not trying to learn techniques for talking to the unconverted or even to gain logical arguments to use in defense of their faith."[3]

I want to make it clear that I believe that every Christian should know how to share the gospel of Jesus Christ in a systematic way. There are some excellent evangelism training methods available today. But after the potential leader has learned the technique (e.g., the outline, the presentation), he or she must build relationships with non-Christians so that after presenting the gospel, the fruit remains.

CONTINUAL CARE

When we were first evaluating the evangelism in our cells, our senior pastor asked us, "How many conversions did you have in your network this week?" We were all a bit confused when one director reported zero, but later said that eight people received Christ in a separate ministry of evangelism which was unconnected with the cell ministry. At that time, we had just begun our cell church transition and a separate program called evangelism remained. During that meeting, we decided that we would make every effort to connect evangelism in the church with cell ministry. We wanted disciples, not just decisions.

Discipleship naturally flows from evangelism in a cell group. After John wins Roy to Christ, John continues to disciple Roy within the context of the cell group.

Program-based churches scramble to find people in the church to "follow up" the newcomers. So many conversions pad the church reports, but yield little long-term fruit. This is not the case for conversions in the cell group. When a person receives Christ in a cell group, he or she is immediately surrounded with fellow pilgrims, making the journey bearable.

WELCOMING NON-CHRISTIANS

"She likes attending my cell group, and yes, she'll eventually become a Christian," René said to me. René's confidence that Mary would eventually receive Jesus was based on the fact that dozens and dozens of people have received Christ through his cell group. René and his wife Patricia welcome non-Christians. They make them feel like family. These non-Christians feel the liberty to share their fears, doubts, and feelings.

On one particular night, I visited René's cell group. I noticed that one couple said very little. When asked to share their thoughts on a biblical passage, it became apparent that they lacked a personal relationship with Jesus Christ. René didn't pounce on them with the Good News. In René's cell group, non-Christians feel comfortable as topics are openly discussed without controversy. René closed the cell by asking anyone to repeat the "sinner's prayer" with him. With the compassion of Christ, René pointed them to the Savior.

Many cell groups not only make non-Christians feel welcome, they make them a priority. Bethany World Prayer Center, for example, asks their cell leaders to open cell groups among their non-Christian friends — wherever they might be.

At the Republic Church, we have over 30 university cell groups, which focus primarily on evangelism. The open-air environment of the university campus lends itself to reaching non-Christians. Johnny Suarez started our first university cell group among non-Christians. In a matter of months, several of the non-Christians received Christ.

Mary Louise, one of those new believers, was soon baptized and started leading a different cell group on the same university campus, with Johnny Suarez supervising. Even though these groups are more seeker sensitive, the components of knowing God and relationship building are still present.

The Church on Brady, an urban church planting ministry, started 12 churches in the heart of Los Angeles. To reach this hardcore, ethnically diverse group, the Church on Brady relied entirely on small groups geared toward non-Christians. Six questions helped focus the small groups around the prescribed Biblical passages:[4]

1. What did you like?
2. What did you not like?
3. What did you not understand?
4. What did you learn about God?
5. What do you want to do in response?
6. What phrase, thought, or sentence would you take home with you?

In these groups there is little praying, singing, or talking about the church. The needs of the non-Christians are the priority.[5] Ralph Neighbour calls them Target Groups because they target a particular audience. Most cell churches simply call them cell groups, while acknowledging their special emphasis. Although the "seeker sensitive" cell caters its message to the unbeliever, it doesn't mean that discipleship is lacking.

CONSISTENT VISITATION

When Nehemiah heard about the terrible state of the temple in Jerusalem, he said, "I sat down and wept. For some days I mourned and fasted and prayed before the God of heaven" (Neh. 1:4). But Nehemiah did more than weep and pray. He acted by presenting his burden to the King and later *visiting* Jerusalem (Neh. 2). He became the solution to his prayers by personally visiting the problem area. One of the best ways for a cell leader to put "feet on his or her prayers" is through personal visitation. Through personal visitation a cell leader truly understands the state of his flock.

When a person starts attending a cell, it's often difficult to know the person's spiritual state. Frank, for example, could speak the Christian lingo, but at times there were indications that he lacked a personal relationship with Jesus Christ. I really didn't know his spiritual state until I visited him personally. It didn't take much probing before I realized that Frank had entered the evangelical faith because of his Christian wife. "I'm trying to become a Christian by growing in knowledge," he told me. I suggested to him that we meet at my house the following week in order to understand the true meaning of Christianity. He received Jesus in my home the following week and continues to grow in His faith.

Cho writes, "I have found the only definite way to increase church membership is through personal contact, . . ."[6] Personal contact, as defined by Cho, involves visiting cell members, recent contacts, personal evangelism, as well as meeting physical needs of hurting people.[7] At Yoido Full Gospel Church, the passion for visitation doesn't merely reside among the paid clergy. The pastors have passed the baton to the lay leaders as well. According to a survey taken among 400 lay leaders, the average cell leader visited three to five households each week.[8]

The 1 $^1/_2$ hours spent during the cell meeting is inadequate to properly care for the flock. A cell leader must also meet with individuals on separate occasions.

In my questionnaire of over 700 cell leaders, I discovered a direct correlation between how often the cell leader contacted new people and his or her success in multiplying the group. If the leader contacted five to seven new people per month, there was an 80 percent chance that he or she would multiply the cell group. When the leader only visited one to three people per month the chances dropped to 60 percent.

I know that it's hard to pick-up the phone and call a cell member or get in the car to make a visit. Often, it takes sheer will power. And perhaps this is what distinguishes successful cell leaders. They do what they know they should do when they know they should do it. Theodore Roosevelt, one of the great leaders of the twentieth century once said, "There is nothing brilliant or outstanding in my record, except this one thing: I do the things that I believe ought to be done . . . And when I make up my mind to do a thing, I act." Contacting your flock requires action, whether you feel like it or not.

Here are some helpful principles that will guide you in your visitation of both newcomers and faithful members of the group. First, visit the cell members systematically. In this way, a cell leader avoids excluding anyone.[9] Second, make the visit brief. Cell leaders can learn from the art of pastoral visitation. A 15-minute visit is sufficient. It's better to depart earlier than later. Leave the person wishing that you could have stayed longer, rather than uncomfortable because you didn't leave earlier. Third, visit strategically. Start with your future cell leaders; next visit the less committed; finally, visit the newcomers to the group.

EFFECTIVE COMMUNICATION

The cell group is all about communication. The cell leader's goal is to stimulate communication, interaction, and participation among the members of the group. Because of this, cell leaders should learn as much as possible about the art of small group dynamics. Listening, for example, is love visibly expressed to group members; so a cell leader must do a lot of it. Leaders must focus on the responses of the members, instead of being preoccupied with their own words — what they have prepared. Drawing out participation is truly an art that takes a lot of practice. Cell leaders should be especially careful not to dominate the cell meeting and to avoid the mini-service syndrome. They should respond positively to each member, seeking to maintain the flow of participation.

PRESS ON

This chapter is designed to provide the starting point. Most people reading this chapter will immediately see their own need, those areas where they don't measure-up. The good news is that we are all in the process and none of us have arrived. Paul's words bring encouragement and instruction: "Not that I have already obtained all this, or have already been made perfect, but I press on to take hold of that for which Christ Jesus took hold of me. Brothers, I do not consider myself yet to have taken hold of it. But one thing I do: Forgetting what is behind and straining toward what is ahead, I press on toward the goal to win the prize for which God has called me heavenward in Christ Jesus" (Philippians 3:12-14).

TRAINING PATTERNS FOR DEVELOPING CELL LEADERS

7

HOW JESUS
DEVELOPED LEADERS

Jesus constantly challenged people to follow Him. I counted more than 25 occasions in the gospels in which Jesus directly exhorted people to come after Him. One of those followers was Peter. Although hesitant at times, Peter followed Jesus all the way to martyrdom. Before his death, he exhorted his own disciples, "To this you were called, because Christ suffered for you, leaving you an example, that you should follow in his steps" (1 Peter 2:21). Paul, another follower of Christ, challenged the church in Corinth to, "Follow my example, as I follow the example of Christ" (1 Corinthians 11:1). Like Peter and Paul, we are called to follow Christ's example.

The principles that Jesus used in training His disciples apply directly to leadership training today. Jesus took a ragtag group of men and transformed them into highly motivated leaders. We would do well to follow His example of leadership training.

JESUS CALLED PEOPLE OUT OF THE CROWD

It's important to remember that Jesus called people out of the crowd, the multitude, to enter into a discipleship relationship with Him. The objective of Christ's ministry among the crowd was to convert the crowd into disciples. Christ's purpose was always to prepare committed followers rather than enthusiasts. When a person made a personal decision to follow Jesus, that person would come out of the crowd and become Christ's disciple.

Cell churches ask the multitude on Sunday morning — the listeners — to enter specific training with the goal of eventually leading a cell group. Cell churches focus on training the masses to become cell leaders. The main goal of the cell church is not how many people attend the Sunday service, but how many new groups will be started. A cell leader has taken on an additional commitment, above and beyond mere church attendance.

JESUS DEMONSTRATED VITAL TRUTHS

Jesus didn't simply teach His disciples about prayer. Rather, he asked them to accompany Him to prayer meetings. He allowed His disciples to see Him praying. When the disciples finally asked Him what He was doing, He seized the opportunity to teach them about prayer (Lk. 11:1-4). Instead of offering a class on hermeneutics or exegesis, Jesus quoted Scripture in his dialogue and then explained the Scripture's meaning to them (66 references to the Old Testament in His dialogue with the disciples). The same is true of evangelism. Jesus evangelized people in the presence of His disciples and then instructed them afterwards. He took advantage of real life situations to carefully explain complex doctrinal issues (e.g., rich young ruler in Mt. 19:23).

Christ was constantly reviewing the experiences of His disciples and then offering additional commentary (Mk. 9:17-29; 6:30-44). Christ's pattern was as follows:

☑ Give the disciples experiences and allow them to make personal observations.

☑ Use the experiences and observations as a starting point to teach a lesson.

Christ knew that theoretical information separated from practical experience would have little lasting value. After Christ's disciples finished their ministry tour, they met with Jesus to discuss what happened. The apostles gathered around Jesus and reported to him all they had done and taught (Mk. 6:30). On another occasion, the disciples reported to Jesus, "Lord, even the demons submit to us in Your name" (Lk.10:17). Jesus seized the opportunity to instruct them further and to offer further guidelines: ". . . do not rejoice that the spirits submit to you, but rejoice that your names are written in heaven" (Lk.10:20).

People learn best by doing. However, they must not be left to themselves. It's essential that they receive personal supervision and guidance to carry on with the work. Supervision forms the building block of cell ministry. Without it, individual cells and cell leaders will start rotating on their own orbits within their own solar systems and will eventually cause grief to the church. With diligent supervision, a new cell leader will learn from his or her mistakes. Supervision in the cell church is the oil that keeps the machinery running.

A clear-cut, well-defined equipping track with excellent material is essential in the cell church. Just as important, however, is the practical demonstration and supervision of the concepts by the cell leader. In the cell church, all potential cell leaders must participate in a cell while receiving informational training. The cell leader, like Jesus, must demonstrate cell principles in the presence of the potential cell leader and even allow him or her to participate in the cell (e.g., lead the icebreaker, etc.).

JESUS CONCENTRATED ON FUTURE LEADERS

Christ knew that He would need to concentrate on specific leaders in order to transform the world. Men, not programs, formed the basis of Christ's outreach to the world. At times, Christ even chose to flee from the crowds in order to concentrate His energies on His disciples, who would eventually lead the Church. Jesus didn't neglect the multitude, but He focused on His disciples who provided supervision and discipleship to the rest. He often took them away from the crowds as we read in Mark 9:30-31: "Jesus did not want anyone to know where they were, because He was teaching His disciples."

Of the 550 verses in Mark that record Christ's ministry, 282 show Jesus relating to the public, while 268 illustrate his working with the twelve.[1] Christ practiced the principle of concentration: the smaller the size of the group, the greater possibility of instruction. Even within the group of 12, He gave more attention to James, Peter, and John. Christ's example instructs us to remember that teaching effectiveness coincides with group size.

How different from the traditional training models that reigned supreme in Christ's day. The scribes followed a scholastic procedure that included strict rituals and formulas of knowledge. Christ, in contrast, asked His disciples to observe His example. Robert Coleman remarks:

When one stops to think of it, this was an incredibly simple way of doing it. Jesus had no formal school, no seminaries, no outlined course of study, no periodic membership classes in which he enrolled his followers. None of these highly organized procedures considered so necessary today entered into his ministry. Amazing as it may seem, all Jesus did to teach these men his way was to draw them close to himself. He was his own school and curriculum.[2]

Christ's intentional concentration on the twelve gains significance when we realize that the multitudes clamored for His attention. They wanted to take Him by force and crown Him King (John 6:15). Even the Pharisees admitted that the world had gone after Him (John 12:19). Yet Christ knew that He needed to focus on the few in order to prepare those who would actually lead the multitude.

We know from the book of Acts that Christ's strategy worked: Acts 2:41-42 says: "Those who accepted his [Peter's] message were baptized, and about three thousand were added to their number that day. They devoted themselves to the apostles' teaching and to the fellowship, to the breaking of bread and to prayer."

Training in cell ministry might include the classroom, but must go beyond it. It must involve personal interaction between trainee and trainer in on-the-job experience. Cell leaders must make personal contact with cell members for lasting fruit to remain. Effective leadership training involves personal attention.

JESUS DEMANDED OBEDIENCE

Jesus demanded obedience from His disciples. Often the disciples didn't understand Christ's words or teaching. They failed to grasp the meaning of Christ's death on the cross (Mt. 16:22), their own place in the kingdom (Mk. 9:33-37), and humble service to others (Mt. 20:24). Yet, Jesus saw that they had a teachable attitude and were willing to learn. Christ's disciples were willing to forsake all to follow Him (Lk. 5:11), and this was the one key ingredient that Christ required.

What characterizes effective leaders today is obedience. Additional knowledge is only given as a result of acting upon present understanding. Successful leaders understand that the amount of knowledge they possess is far less important than what they do with it.

JESUS EXPECTED HIS LEADERS TO REPRODUCE

Christ's last command to His disciples clarifies the goal of His training. He expected His disciples to reproduce in their own disciples the same principles that he taught them. He commanded them to ". . . make disciples of all nations, baptizing them in the name of the Father and of the Son and of the Holy Spirit, and teaching them to obey everything I have commanded you" (Mt. 28:19-20).

FOLLOWING CHRIST'S PATTERN

The cell church comes close to the biblical discipleship method of Jesus. There isn't an exact comparison, but commonality abounds. That same passion that governed Christ's life in the training of the 12 must compel the cell leader to spot, develop, and release new cell leadership. A cell leader has made a commitment to stand apart from the crowd, making a higher-level commitment to Jesus Christ. These are the true disciples in any church and should be recognized as such. The great churches go one step further and make it their goal to send forth an entire army of cell leaders.

8

Developing a
Mentoring System

Can you remember someone who has had a lasting, caring impact on your life? One high school class in Harlem in New York City remembers Eugene Lang in a very special way. Lang was asked to speak to 60 high school students at his alma mater, Public School 121. The president of a highly successfully venture capital firm, Lang knew that less than 50% of the students would ever graduate from high school. He once sat in the same classroom and knew the rocky road the students would face.

When he spoke to those kids in 1981, he set before them an amazing offer: He offered to pay for the college education of each student who graduated from high school. Lang did more than offer a freebie; he invested personal time and attention in those 60 kids.[1] As a result, 52 of the 60 students graduated from P.S. 121 and 34 went on to college. Lang empowered the students in that class to success by getting involved, by becoming part of his speech. Mentoring in its purest sense is empowering others to succeed.

What is Mentoring?

The word *mentor* originated in Greek mythology. Mentor was the name of a wise and faithful advisor to Odysseus. When Odysseus left for a long voyage, he entrusted the teaching of his son Telemachus to his advisor, Mentor. Through the counsel of Mentor, Odysseus's son became a great leader.[2] Mentoring describes someone in relationship with someone else. This relationship might be formal, informal, intensive, or occasional. The mentor might not even know that he or she is mentoring. The best explanation of mentoring that I've found comes from Dr. Robert Clinton who defines mentoring as a " . . . relational experience in which one person empowers another by sharing God-given resources."[3]

Mentoring Encompasses a Variety of Relationships

The concept of mentoring is so refreshing because of its wide application. If you're like me, you can't point to just one person who influenced your life. You'll probably point to many who mentored you at different periods in your life. God in His grace provides mentors throughout our lives to strengthen and encourage us.

Mentoring is not discipleship, although it includes discipleship. The main difference is the scope of the two terms. Discipleship is more narrowly focused, emphasizing the spiritual dimensions of the person. Many understand discipleship to involve an intentional, formal, and regular relationship with someone (especially younger Christians).

Mentoring, on the other, is a far broader expression that goes beyond discipleship. Mentoring might be occasional, informal, or historical. In the following chart, Clinton describes how mentoring might include active discipleship, occasional counseling, or can even be done vicariously through the reading of biographies.[4] Depending on the type of relationship, a mentor might fulfill the role of teacher, coach, sponsor, friend, counselor, or advisor.

VARIOUS TYPES OF MENTORING[5]

ACTIVE	OCCASIONAL	PASSIVE
Discipler A mature follower of Christ helping an immature Christian to grow in the Christian habits. **Spiritual Director** A spiritual person developing a person who needs to develop spiritually. **Coach** A relational process, in which a person who knows how to do something very well, imparts that capacity to someone who desires to learn.	**Counselor** Very much like a normal counselor. One finds formalized counselors who make a profession of helping the body of Christ through counseling. There are others who counsel on a more informal basis. **Teacher** This is your normal gifted teacher who teaches knowledge to people with a specific need to learn who are motivated by the teacher to put their knowledge into action. **Sponsor** This is a person with influence who lifts up a young, emerging leader. He might do this by encouraging him/her or recommending him/her.	**Contemporary Model** An attraction to follow a person who has gifts like our own. **Historical Model** A person can be mentored vicariously through the study of someone's life in biographical form. **Divine Contact** God sometimes sends along a divine contact to mentor us in some special way whether we want it or not. We should be prepared to recognize him and respond accordingly to God's empowerment through him.

You might complain that you can't find a mentor. Have you tried reading biographies of godly men and women of the past? Historical mentors can have a powerful impact on our lives. C.T. Studd stimulated me to become a missionary. George Mueller on more than one occasion has challenged my faith. Mentoring also occurs through sponsoring, counseling, teaching, and peer relationships, to name a few.

The Sponsor Mentor

A sponsor is a mentor that knows something that you don't, or who can open a door that you can't. The role of a sponsor is to use expert knowledge and experience to help someone else who lacks that expertise.

Consider the strategic role that Barnabas played in the life of the apostle Paul . No one in Jerusalem wanted to associate with Paul. Why risk your life? Barnabas possessed something that Paul needed — a special relationship with the "top brass" in Jerusalem. As a true sponsor, Barnabas presented Paul to his doubting friends, thus cementing Paul's ministry with the pillars of the New Testament church. The writer of Acts notes, "But Barnabas took him and brought him to the apostles. He told them how Saul on his journey had seen the Lord and that the Lord had spoken to him, and how in Damascus he had preached fearlessly in the name of Jesus. So Saul stayed with them and moved about freely in Jerusalem, speaking boldly in the name of the Lord" (Acts 9:27-28).

The Counseling Mentor

Mentoring is broad enough to include a word of counsel, an insight, or an encouragement. Think of the counsel that Jethro gave Moses. It came from a true friend and at just the right moment, thus revolutionizing Moses' ministry. Solomon said, "Make plans by seeking advice; if you wage war, obtain guidance" (Proverbs 20:18). True mentors stay alert for counseling opportunities so that young leaders avoid making serious misjudgments. Clinton says, "Informal one-time mentoring encounters can protect young leaders from actions that would have serious consequences."[6]

My wife, Celyce, and I experienced such an informal one-time counsel in 1988. At that time, Celyce and I were planning on spending the rest of our lives in Guinea, West Africa as missionaries with the Christian and Missionary Alliance. When we mentioned this to Don Young, the candidate secretary of the C&MA, he gave us a disapproving look and encouraged us to consider South America. He figured that at 32 years of age, I would have a hard time learning the two required languages of Guinea, West Africa.

We were crushed by his advice but decided to consider his words. After all, he was the boss. We browsed the various Latin American countries in Patrick Johnston's *Operation World,* noting that Ecuador would be a good choice with evangelicals comprising only 3.5% of the national population. The bottom line was that we weren't sure. Even after fasting and praying, we remained doubtful. On the second day of fasting, we received a letter from Paul Johnson, a missionary in Ecuador, with the precise word of counsel we needed. We hadn't talked to this missionary for at least 1 $1/2$ years, so we know that God supernaturally stirred him to send a letter at just the right time. Here's what his letter said:

> Are you still thinking of Africa for missionary work? It is great if you are. But in all fairness to you, I think you should find out what God says to you when you ask Him specifically about Ecuador. We have so much opportunity here with several very "going" churches. With your experience, you would do well in a team ministry in the city of your choice. I would never want to influence you one way or another but sure wouldn't mind if the good Lord would head you in this direction.

It was a word of counsel that met our needs at the right time in our lives. Paul Johnson decided to pick up his pen and write to a young pastor who needed direction. This is the heart of mentoring — making the effort to speak into the life of a potential leader.

The Peer Mentor

Sometimes we think that a mentoring relationship is one-way. I mentor you and you mentor someone else. This is not always the case. Peer mentoring can also take place among those of the same age and the same maturity level. Jonathan and David mentored each other through a rock solid friendship. Kevin Strong and I have a similar relationship. We are peer mentors. When we meet together, we share our stories. I listen to his struggles, and he listens to mine. The greatest benefits of our peer mentoring relationships occur in the listening process. We don't try to hide anything. In fact, we make it a point to share deep struggles. When I do offer advice to Kevin, I try not to sound dogmatic. The best counseling in a peer mentoring relationship is the empathy that comes from being heard. We always end our time in prayer. When Kevin was recently diagnosed with brain cancer for the second time, he knew that he could count on me for empathy and prayer.

ELEMENTS OF THE MENTORING RELATIONSHIP

Role Modeling

Paul tells us to follow his example. He says in 1 Corinthians 11:1: "Follow my example, as I follow the example of Christ." To the Thessalonians, he said, "For you yourselves know how you ought to follow our example" (2 Thess. 3:7). A mentor is foremost an example. Jesus didn't yell to us from heaven. No, he came down in the form of a man and lived among us. He modeled how we should live. As Howard Hendricks says, "God always wraps His truth in a person. That's the value of a godly mentor. He shows what biblical truth looks like with skin on it."[7]

I was fortunate to have Peter Wagner as my Ph.D. mentor in a formal way, but Peter Wagner also mentored me informally. The most memorable times I experienced were when I worked as Peter's research assistant. While sitting in his office, I observed the order of his books, the way he worked, his plaques, etc. It was the richest education I received while at Fuller Theological Seminary. I still consider Peter Wagner my mentor and model, although we rarely talk personally. He continues to have a lasting impact on my life.

Whether we like it or not, our lives are a living model to those around us. Some will want to emulate our example. This is the role of a *contemporary mentor*. A contemporary mentor ministers to people through his or her role model, whether there is an intentional, formal relationship or not. Contemporary mentors live out values we hold important and stir us to follow their example. Albert Bandura, the renowned psychologist who taught for many years at Stanford University, believes that most human behavior is learned observationally through modeling.[8] Medical missionary Albert Schweitzer once said, "Example is not the main thing in influencing others . . . it is the only thing."

Attraction

People will try to live up to the expectations of those they admire and respect. Finding the right mentor is somewhat like being in love. A certain chemistry must be present. Many mentoring relationships fail because of lack of attraction. It's this attraction element that stirs a person to work hard to please the mentor. There's a desire to bend over backwards to fulfill the requirements that the mentor demands. Normally the person being mentored is attracted to the mentor because of the knowledge and resources that the mentor possesses. In other words, the person being mentored desires to possess what the mentor has. The mentor empowers his mentoree by sharing God-given resources.

Relationship

Paul, the apostle, often referred to his disciples by endearing names, such as "dear son" (Timothy). If you know someone who cares for you and wants you to succeed, most likely you'll be motivated to excel.

The mentor should strive to establish friendship and trust in the mentoring relationship. Open sharing and transparency cement relationships; therefore, the mentor must openly share his or her life and struggles. In *The Art of Mentoring,* Shirley Peddy says:

> Tell your story first. So often we make the mistake of asking the other person a question, and putting him on the spot. How did you like the meeting this morning? Did you stay until it ended?" This is more an interrogation than a "trust" builder. No wonder the other person feels exposed and vulnerable. He wonders why you are asking. How should he answer? Is this a test? To avoid this reaction, always start with your own story, making sure it isn't something that puts you in a highly favorable light. Maybe when you attended the meeting in the morning, you slipped out a few minutes early. "I can never stay awake in meetings anyway," you tell him. By disclosing something personal about yourself, you take the initial step toward creating trust.[9]

Mentoring, then, first involves a caring relationship. Great mentors listen well. They realize that those they mentor desire to share their life goals and dreams. They understand that listening is hard work and they prepare themselves accordingly.

Accountability

To avoid disappointment in mentoring, it's best to place everything on the table at the beginning of a mentoring relationship.

Individuals need to talk openly about such questions as the frequency of meetings, assignments, material used, and when the mentoring will terminate. Unlike parenting relationships, mentoring will run its course.

For mentoring to work, the mentoree must demonstrate an attitude of voluntary submission so that advice and assignments will be respected and fulfilled.[10] This "responsiveness" is reflected in Paul's advice to Timothy: "And the things you have heard me say in the presence of many witnesses entrust to reliable men who will also be qualified to teach others"(2 Tim. 2:2).

John (not his real name) seemed like a great guy to mentor. He made a point to seek me out, and I felt equally attracted to minister to him. We spent lots of time together, both formally and informally. On various occasions, I invited John to dinner at our home. My children eagerly looked forward to John's visits. Everything seemed to click, until I noticed a fatal flaw.

I discovered that John didn't follow through on commitments. He would say *yes* to my suggestions in order to please me, but then failed to act. I desired honesty more than blind obedience, but I expected him to keep his word. I noticed that failure to keep his word was a pattern in his life, and eventually I was forced to cut off the mentoring relationship. John continues to wander through life, seeking work here and there with little success. Suffice it to say, commitment, faithfulness, and follow through are essential qualifications in the mentoring relationship.

If a mentor enters an intense, formal relationship with a mentoree, he or she should expect results. In *Coaching: Evoking Excellence in Others,* James Flaherty says, ". . . it's invalid for a coach to say, 'I did everything right, but the coaching didn't work.' My view is that a coach who makes that statement wasn't correcting as he went along, and instead followed a rote routine that may have worked before."[11] The mentor or coach should adjust the process according to the results and be willing to learn afresh in each situation.

MENTORING IN THE CELL CHURCH

Many cell churches connect each new believer in the cell with a mentor/sponsor from within the same cell group. Mark Jobe, pastor of New Life Community Church, sailed along on the success of multiplying cell groups until he realized that mentoring in the cells was lacking. He writes: "In our early cell group days, we made the mistake of assuming that disciple-making would take place by simply bringing people together in cells. Now we know that we were missing a key link in the discipleship process — one-on-one sponsoring (mentoring) within the cell context. Now we know people need to be trained to sponsor others in Christ. It doesn't happen automatically."[12]

The cell leader must take the responsibility to make sure that each newcomer receives discipleship. It's better if a member of the group is assigned to the newcomer so that the responsibility is shared within the group. The cell leader should attempt to connect people of the same age, gender, and any other common characteristics, although the element of attraction (mentioned above) might not always be possible.

Often a mentor-sponsor will use a study guide to lead the weekly discussion, but above all he must trust the guidance of the Holy Spirit. The mentor's goal is to guide the newcomer to maturity, with the ultimate goal of preparing the person to lead a cell group.

But mentoring is never an end in itself. Rather, it's one link in the chain. The mentor spends enough time with the new convert to pass him or her along to the next link. Future links in the chain include leadership training and deployment (i.e., leading his or her own cell). The chain is not complete until the new cell leader is also spotting, training, and releasing new leaders to direct their own groups.

In most equipping tracks the initial mentor does not do all of the training. He or she only begins the process and then passes the new convert on to the next step. A pastor, zone supervisor, or G-12 leader will often equip the potential leader. These anointed teachers must include mentoring in their equipping by offering counsel, sponsoring, and building relationships with the potential leader.

9

STRATEGIES FOR
DEVELOPING LEADERS

In the battle, soldiers have little room for lofty theories. They want weapons and communications that work. The Marines, for example, have chosen a handheld communications device based on its ruggedness in battle. General Cummiskey demonstrated the roughness of this device by throwing it on the ground and stomping on it during the 1997 COMDEX conference.[1] Theory is great for the lab and classroom, but in the real world people desire something that works.

Leadership theories abound, but only a few actually work in the real battle of life. After reviewing the last 50 years of leadership theory, some of the discoveries caused me to sit up and listen, while others seemed no more than interesting laboratory experiments that failed the test of real life. I believe that the following leadership strategies will help you to lead others more effectively.

SITUATIONAL LEADERSHIP

According to situational leadership, a leader's style is dictated by the needs of the followers. Simply put, there is no single style of leadership that will always be effective — it all depends on the maturity level of the follower. Effective leaders size up the maturity level of the follower and then lead accordingly.

If the follower is a brand new Christian, for example, an effective leader will offer clear-cut advice about exactly how to proceed in the Christian life. If the follower were a mature Christian, the leader would use a gentler, more non-directive approach. According to *situational leadership,* the effectiveness of the leader is determined by how well he or she sizes up the situation and then applies the correct leadership style to meet the needs of his followers in that particular situation.[2]

This approach has helped me tremendously in my ministry. I've learned to analyze each one of my followers and lead accordingly. For the cell leaders I oversee, for example, I must adjust my style of leadership according to the person I'm leading.

Vinicio is a self-starter who runs his own business. He and his wife Patricia desire to follow Jesus above all else. I've pastored Vinicio and Patricia since 1992 when they first started leading a cell group. I've learned that Vinicio responds best to a *hands-off* leadership style. I delegate a lot to Vinicio, knowing that he's a mature follower. I would fail miserably with Vinicio and Patricia by exercising too much authority or demanding that they perform certain tasks.

Michael, another cell leader I oversee, is not a self-starter. His intentions are worthy, but he doesn't always follow through on his commitments. Although mature spiritually, he lacks motivation for many tasks in life. I've discovered that the best approach to leadership with Michael is the direct approach. I need to spell out exactly what I want him to do and then supervise him closely to make sure he follows through on his commitment. Michael needs a more direct style of leadership.

Jesus exercised situational leadership with His 12 apostles.[3] At first Jesus exercised more control, but as the maturity level of his followers increased, he delegated more authority to them. Christ finally left the church in their hands, considering the disciples fully capable of leading His Church. Icenogle writes, "Empirical research of small group behavior has affirmed the relationship between group growth and maturity and aggressive leadership styles. The highly directive early leadership style of Jesus among the Twelve transitioned into a final and completely delegating style."[4]

Some leaders feel they have to be the strong, authoritative leader at all times (e.g., the Latin American *caudillo*-style of leadership). Because this type of leader doesn't adjust his leadership style, many of the mature, highly competent followers leave the church. Why? Because they don't feel valued, respected, and appreciated. It's as if their opinion didn't matter. *Situational leadership* reminds us that if the follower is competent and highly motivated, the leader needs to show respect and support, rather than dictating every decision.

Other leaders are overly democratic — you could even say wimpy, tossed with the winds and the waves. These leaders must take heed to the challenge of *situational leadership* and behave in a directive, authoritarian style when the situation calls for it.

The key to success is to size-up the situation and to exercise the leadership style that the situation demands. When Celyce and I first arrived on the mission field, we were assigned to a missionary couple that acted as big brothers. This sincere couple poured out their hearts on our behalf, but they failed to take into account our years of pastoral experience and missionary training before coming to Ecuador. They tried to tell us what to do each step of the way, just like the previous missionaries who needed more control. Unlike the missionaries before us, we longed for a hands-off style of leadership, one that would have respected our knowledge and background.

Effective leaders are constantly seeking to determine what style of leadership works best in each particular situation. For immature followers, an effective leader will establish time-lines, set specific goals, help organize the follower's behavior, and tell the person what to do and exactly how to do it. If the follower is a self-starter, a quick-learner and works well on his or her own, the leader will use a non-directive style of leadership. The leader will engage in more two-way communication, facilitation, listening, and providing feedback. The great thing about *situational leadership* is that it does not prescribe only one kind of leadership style. It says that an effective leader must adjust his or her style to the needs of the follower. The following chart depicts the various leadership styles that you might use, depending on the maturity of your followers.

SITUATIONAL LEADERSHIP[5]

3 HIGH RELATIONSHIP LOW TASK *Share ideas and facilitate in decision making* **PARTICIPATING**	HIGH RELATIONSHIP 2 HIGH TASK *Explain decisions and provide opportunity for clarification* SELLING
4 LOW RELATIONSHIP LOW TASK *Turn over responsibility for decisions and implementation* **DELEGATING**	LOW RELATIONSHIP 1 HIGH TASK *Provide specific instructions and closely supervise performance* TELLING

SHEPHERD VERSUS RANCHER

The Shepherd/Rancher concept was first coined by Lyle E. Schaller.[6] This paradigm has many similarities to the Jethro model, but is easier to grasp — especially for pastors who are trying to pastor their congregations on their own. The background is the real world of shepherds and ranchers. The idea centers on how a shepherd cares for individual sheep while a rancher cares for those who are caring for the sheep. A shepherd of a single flock of sheep gives individual attention to each of the sheep in the flock. Such a shepherd is limited by his physical capacity to care for the sheep. A rancher, in contrast, has a number of shepherds under his care who do the actual shepherding of the flock. Both the shepherd and the rancher care for the sheep; the difference is that one does the actual caring, and the other administrates those who do the caring.

Most pastors in North America behave like pastors of individual flocks. They feel responsible to care for each and every person under them. The problem is that a single pastor can only physically and spiritually care for so many sheep before the task becomes unmanageable. How many people can an individual pastor truly care for? Some would say up to 200 people.[7] Carl George, however, disagrees. He says:

> The underlying assumption behind these attitudes is that a pastor or skilled lay leader can provide adequate care for a group of 50-100. In reality, he or she cannot. What actually transpires is a limited intimacy and a limited accountability. Over time, many people grow dissatisfied and disillusioned, not understanding why it's so hard to go deeper in feelings of caring and belonging.[8]

Even if an individual pastor thinks that he can care for an entire congregation, in reality he or she cannot provide adequate care for the entire flock. If a pastor tries to care for the entire church by himself, studies have proven that the church is not likely to grow beyond two hundred people. Peter Wagner says, "But in order to get through the

200 barrier and sustain a healthy rate of growth, the pastor must be willing to pay a price too high for some: he or she must be willing to shift from a shepherd mode to a rancher mode."[9]

To better understand the transition process from pastor to rancher, it is helpful to examine the characteristics of both. The following table helps us to see the differences:[10]

CHARACTERISTICS OF A PASTOR
VERSUS A RANCHER

TRADITIONAL PASTOR-SHEPHERD	RANCHER
☑ Tries to personally satisfy all of the needs. ☑ Believes that he is responsible for everything. ☑ Participates in every meeting. ☑ Depends on the compliments of others. ☑ Does not delegate much. ☑ Vision is limited by what he can do. ☑ Sees the congregation as individuals and not as groups of people. ☑ Does not possess clear church growth goals for the church.	☑ Focuses on small groups to care for the church. ☑ Is the leader of the church and is not afraid of making changes. ☑ Delegates with flexibility. Is more concerned with the results than the process. ☑ Is able to say NO to ministry opportunities, if there is someone else that can do it. ☑ Creates roles for the congregation to fill. ☑ Wants the people to be free from dependence upon him. ☑ Is an excellent administrator. Reserves time for planning and prayer. ☑ Raises up and trains the leaders of small groups.

There are several key changes that must be made if a pastor is going to transition into the role of a rancher. First, there must be the willingness to pastor the church through other people. This involves trusting people and delegating responsibility to them. Today's ranchers, or large church pastors, must pastor their people through under-shepherds.

A second major change is to focus on training lay people to do the work of the ministry. This is scriptural. Paul says in Ephesians 4: 11,12, "It was he who gave some . . . to be pastors and teachers, to prepare God's people for works of service, so that the body of Christ may be built up." According to these verses, a pastor's role is to train others to do the work of the ministry. The true rancher will spend the majority of his time training others.[11]

The rancher paradigm is uniquely suited for cell ministry today. The goal of the pastor whose church is based on cells is to pastor those who are pastoring the church. In the cell church, the senior pastor does not even attempt to develop face-to-face, pastoral relationships with individual members of the congregation. Rather, he is committed to meeting face-to-face with those who are caring for the congregation.[12] This is why it is not uncommon to hear of cell churches that have between 10,000 and 200,000 people. In these churches there is a care system that touches lives in a personal way.

The cell church pastor is a pure rancher. He spends his best time with leaders who will pastor the flock. He's not as concerned with attendance as he is with available small group leadership, knowing that the attendance will come when there is available leadership. The major goal for this type of pastor is how many cell groups will be functioning in the church. He knows that if he can mobilize the laity to lead cell groups, the flock will feel the necessary personal care.

LEADERSHIP EMERGENCE

If you know that God has been developing your leadership ability over a lifetime, you'll most likely stay for the whole ride. No one understands this better than Dr. J. Robert Clinton, who has dedicated his life to studying the principles and patterns of great leaders. After studying and analyzing more than 1,300 prominent leaders, Clinton developed a discipline called emergence theory.[13] Emergence theory identifies common patterns that God repeatedly uses in developing the life of a leader. Clinton has developed useful tools to aid students in determining their own leadership emergence. Emerging leaders normally pass through five stages:

- *Sovereign Foundations:* In this phase, God is working in the leader's personality to make the leader the person God wants him or her to be.

- *Inner-Life Growth:* Usually, in this stage, the leader receives training. Those who feel a special call to the ministry will often attend Bible school, theological education by extension, or other forms of specialized training.

- *Ministry Maturing:* In this stage, the leader gains needed ministry experience. This is often more incidental than intentional. Like the first two stages, God is more interested in the development of the leader.

- *Life Maturing:* In this stage, the leader identifies his or her gift-mix and uses it with power. This is a period in which giftedness emerges along with priorities.

- *Convergence:* In this stage, everything flows together: gift-mix, location, experience, and temperament. Clinton says, "Not many leaders experience convergence. Often they are promoted to roles that hinder their gift-mix."[14] He goes on to say, "Leaders have a tendency to cease developing once they have some skills and ministry experience. They may be content to continue their ministry as is, without discerning the need to develop further."[15]

One of the key concepts in Clinton's emergence theory is how God uses trials to mold and shape us. All leaders can point to critical incidents (i.e., watershed events, decisive moments, etc.) when God taught them something very important. Upon successful completion of the ministry task, the leader is usually given a bigger task. Some of these shaping activities include:

- *Obedience test* — God will often test a leader in the area of obedience. Will the leader listen to God's voice and obey? A leader who repeatedly demonstrates that God speaks to him gains spiritual authority and respect from his followers. Having learned to discern God's direction for his own life in numerous crucial decisions, he can then shift to the leadership function of determining guidance for the group that he leads.

- *Submission test* — A developing leader will usually struggle with someone who is in authority over him. Learning submission is critical to learning what authority is, so emerging leaders must first learn to submit. Clinton says, "An important thing to keep in mind is that the ultimate assignment is from God, even if the ministry task is self-initiated or assigned by another."[16]

The development of a leader is first and foremost a God-given endeavor. God is preparing future leaders, placing divine shaping activities and situations in their path. Understanding this perspective reminds us that God is more interested in our leadership development than we are. It helps us to see the diverse circumstances in our lives as coming from His sovereign hand.

We must be faithful in the little things in order to expect greater things. A cell leader must first be faithful in leading a cell group before expecting a greater challenge. I remember one leader in our church that claimed to have a missionary call to the unreached Muslims of North Africa. We asked her to lead a cell group. She initially led the group with excitement but within a few months became very discouraged when she didn't see increased attendance and a harvest of souls. She began to constantly complain and threatened to close the group unless we provided her with more people. She finally closed her group. During my final talk with her I seriously challenged her missionary calling. I told her that missionary work in North Africa would demand more self-initiative, perseverance, and dependence on God through tough times.

Some cell churches even ask their future missionaries to first become cell pastors (leader of leaders) before going overseas. This is a smart move. In the cell church, a leader must first successfully lead a group, multiply it, and then successfully supervise new leaders before applying for higher-level pastoral positions. Churches that cheat on this process will reap their own fruit. Seeing our lives from God's sovereign perspective is a liberating truth that has direct application to leadership in the cell church.

APPLY IT TO YOUR SITUATION

I was quite satisfied to read in a leading computer magazine that the virus checker I currently use has detected and isolated every virus given to it. Detecting and isolating viruses is much more than theory to me now. In the past year, I've accidentally opened seven infected files. Each time, my virus checker came to life and saved me untold agony.

All of the above leadership strategies have worked wonders for me when I needed them most, just like my virus checker. They've made powerful inroads into my own life and ministry over the years. I recommend them to you as you focus on developing and releasing leadership in your own situation. My hope is that these strategies will provide the same exciting results in your ministry.

10

GUIDELINES FOR TRAINING
CELL LEADERS TO
REAP THE HARVEST

God's plan: "Moses, I want you to lead my people out of Egypt."
Excuse #1: "No, God, they won't listen."

God's encouragement: "Moses, I'll perform miracles to help them
listen. In fact, I'll show you those miracles right now."

Excuse #2: "God, I can't speak very well. I feel inadequate."

God's answer: "I will help you speak and will teach you what to
say" (Exodus 4:12).

Like most of us, Moses found reasons to excuse himself from
leadership. None of us are exempt from deep-seated concerns about
our leadership effectiveness. Most leaders in the Bible felt inadequate
and unprepared at the time of their calling. Moses, Isaiah, and the
apostle John were overcome with a sense of inadequacy when they met
God. Even after the initial call, most leaders will find some weakness
to excuse themselves. Thankfully, God sees beyond our inadequacies
and even uses them to strengthen us in ministry.

Words of encouragement to the potential leader will improve the situation but they won't correct it. As you approach prospective leaders, you'll discover that they feel inadequate about their leadership abilities and the amount of training they've received. The first step, therefore, in recruiting potential small group leaders is to assure them that they will receive sufficient training. Leadership training is the surest way to help your new leaders gain confidence.

In the cell church, leadership training is essential. Without it there is no way to sustain quality growth. Those cell churches that are able to raise up leadership quickly and effectively maintain both the quantitative and qualitative edge.

TRAINING FOR A SPECIFIC PURPOSE

Education is a lifelong process. Training, on the other hand, touches specific skills and lasts a limited time. Neil F. McBride, Ed.D., Ph.D., makes a helpful clarification:

> Education is an expanding activity; starting with where a person is at, it provides concepts and information for developing broader perspectives and the foundations for making future analysis and decisions. On the other hand, training is a narrowing activity; given whatever a person's present abilities are, it attempts to provide specific skills and the necessary understanding to apply those skills. The focus is on accomplishing a specific task or job.[1]

McBride's insight about training being a *narrowing activity* versus the *lifetime process* of education touches the nerve of cell leadership training. Understanding the specific purpose of training will help you focus on training potential cell leaders while not ignoring the general on-the-job education that leaders need over the long haul.

EVERYONE ENTERS THE TRAINING TO BECOME A CELL LEADER

When a church concludes that every cell member is a potential cell leader, the logical step is to train each person to lead a cell group eventually. The International Charismatic Mission declares that the goal of the church is for every member to lead in the freedom of Christ, not just to sit watching others do the ministry. As soon as a new convert starts attending ICM, he or she is placed on the training path that ends in cell leadership. Involvement at ICM means entering the equipping track. Ralph Neighbour writes, "Cell churches must take seriously the need to equip every incoming cell member. Cell members will stagnate who are simply invited to attend cells, without clear equipping for service."[2]

LEARNING WHILE DOING

"How do adults learn best?" Most of us would agree that we learn best when the education is personally meaningful — when the learning involves truth that is immediately applied to life. For example, if I own a personal computer and have struggled with word processing, a course on personal computing will whet my appetite and meet an immediate need.

This type of *hands-on* learning is called the problem-solving method of learning. It tries to apply knowledge to areas of immediate need. The sequence for this method: assign, do, and teach. First, there is an assignment that requires my involvement (boot-up the computer, open a document, write a letter, save it, and turn off the computer). Later, I receive feedback, new knowledge, and another assignment. Experience shows that adults learn best if you can get them first to commit to an assignment.

The U.S. Navy uses the "assign, do, teach" procedure (another name for problem-solving method). When learning to swim, for example, everyone is dumped out of the boat and given explicit instructions — get to shore. Those who can't make it are enrolled in a swimming course. The next week the same process is repeated until everyone passes.[3]

The educational sequence, on the other hand, is teach, assign, and do. Students learn lots of information that they will apply sometime in the future. Again, this is a lifetime process because there is so much we need to learn. Learning, in fact, never ends.

Many churches unintentionally follow the educational sequence of training. Why? Because our lifetime education cycle follows this pattern. We naturally apply the techniques that we learned in school to the training of Christian leadership.

Effective cell churches follow the assign, do, and teach method of learning. Potential leaders have the opportunity to serve while receiving training. By taking incremental, practical steps in leading parts of the cell, the trainee develops a hunger to learn more. This process continues until the trainee is actually leading a cell group. Many cell churches continue the process all the way to fulltime ministry.

For example, I allowed Paul to lead parts of my Thursday night cell until eventually he was even leading the Word or edification time. I made it a point to talk with him after the lesson. For the most part, I showered Paul with compliments, but I also interjected specific suggestions to fine-tune his leadership. While Paul was practically involved in the leadership of the cell, he was also receiving training in the equipping track. Paul eventually started his own cell group while maintaining contact with me. Jesus used this method with his disciples. He spent loads of time with them, and they developed confidence in their own ministry by learning and doing ministry with Him. Later the disciples knew how to behave before their persecutors. Peter could say, "For we cannot help speaking about what we have seen and heard" (Acts 4:20). Carl George says: "Many Christians have accepted an absolutely stupid notion: that a person can be lectured into leadership. Leader behaviors, by definition, require followers. Leadership formation cannot occur without on-the-job coaching by someone to whom the leadership trainee is willing to be responsible. Speeches on leader traits will never produce the harvest God wants to grant."[4]

The model of Jesus can be broken down into four simple steps:

- I do — you watch
- I do — you assist
- You do — I assist
- You do — I watch

If you're the parent cell leader, allow your intern to watch you and then explain what you did, and why you did it. Next, observe the intern as he or she does the same thing and objectively explain strengths and weaknesses that you have observed. You must then provide remedial activity to strengthen the weaknesses. More and more you must turn tasks over to the intern while you withdraw, using "benign neglect" as your strategy. You must remain a close friend while treating the intern as your equal.

CLEAR TRAINING FOCUS

I've discovered that the best leadership training courses have a clear-cut beginning and ending. In other words, there is a place to start and a place to finish. Potential leaders graduate and begin leading. The fuzziness is removed. But I've also discovered that many traditional training programs lack a goal. The object, although not stated, is to teach people information with the hope that they will do something with the knowledge later — make their own decision to lead a group, for example. Paul Benjamin, criticizing the North American Sunday School, writes, ". . . this is a school from which no one ever graduates."[5]

"Helter-skelter" training takes place when the church establishes one general educational program and expects all members and potential leaders to follow it. While the intentions are excellent, far too many people fall through the cracks. There is no easy way to track the progress of those passing through this type of system. Thus, few know who has been trained, what type of training has taken place, and who the future cell leaders will be. As a result of the fuzziness, many candidates drop out. Getting lost in the educational machinery is a recurring flaw in the "general education" approach to leadership training.

The most effective cell churches design their training with a clear beginning and ending. The goal is to prepare the new convert to become a cell leader. After becoming a cell leader, there is graduate level training for the person.

The training itself relates to the cell structure. It is not a separate department with a different administration. The training system and the cell ministry "fit like a glove." They are one. In many cell churches the training begins in the cell (mentor-mentoree) because everyone in the church participates in a cell group. In other cell churches, although all new converts are immediately connected with a cell, most of the cell training takes place within the church under the zones or homogeneous departments (e.g., the International Charismatic Mission).

LIMIT THE REQUIREMENTS

Jesus and the apostles bypassed seminary. They failed to meet the educational and ecclesiastical requirements that would have credentialed them to be priests within Judaism. The early Christian movement exploded and developed without regard to any set-apart priesthood.[6]

Many churches pile on years of Christian education before a person can lead a small group, supposing that this is the only way to train leaders. These churches often lose the initial zeal of a young Christian's leadership through an endless maze of requirements. Such churches put out people's fire by over-training them in long, drawn-out courses before they get to actually minister.

Maybe your church isn't so demanding, but you'll have to admit that it's exceedingly easy to add requirement after requirement, course after course, and time commitment after time commitment to leadership training. When we first began planning our equipping track, some members of the pastoral team wanted to include all kinds of courses (e.g., various theology courses, evangelism courses, spiritual warfare). Such an equipping track looked impressive on paper, but it wasn't doable. We realized that our people would get lost in the maze and very few would ever complete it.

I believe in Bible training as well as education in general. But I also know that people learn best when they're involved. If you force them to wait too long before leading a cell group because of endless requirements, the learning experience will diminish.

The key word here is balance. Too much training can frustrate busy volunteers while too little training will make people feel isolated, unprepared, and likely to abandon ship at the earliest opportunity.

MAKE IT DOABLE

One of the most important factors is whether or not the leadership training is doable. Feasibility must guide cell leadership development. Will the potential cell leaders actually graduate from the program? Do you know when they will graduate? How many? Are the requirements too rigid? Are the options too few? If there is only one night available for the training, for example, expect fewer results.

Feasibility also applies to the execution of the training plan. Some of the case study cell churches administered the same educational program for both cell leaders and church members. These churches lumped everyone together, hoping that cell leaders would eventually emerge. The effective cell churches, on the other hand, prepared a specialized training track for cell leaders and excelled at taking the potential leader from point A to point B. In these churches there was a constant supply of available cell leadership.

I remember the early condition of the training program in the El Batán Church, where I first ministered. Our small-group cell leadership training program was meshed with the general educational ministry of the church. On one occasion the pastoral team spent the whole day charting the educational process for all members in our church. We decided that potential leaders — of any kind of ministry — had to follow about four levels of our Bible Academy (a sophisticated name for adult Sunday School).

Everything appeared immaculate on paper. We had solved our problems, theoretically. Our proud system failed because it wasn't doable or "trackable." We let it die, all by itself.

Through experiences like the one I just described, I've learned that feasibility is at the center of cell leadership training. The successful cell churches know nothing of fuzziness and fog in leadership training. The track is clear, and many have boarded the train. There is nothing fuzzy about their leadership training models. The best equipping tracks include:

- ☑ Clear place to start
- ☑ Clear knowledge about where to go
- ☑ Clear idea of victory (leading a cell group)

This is very different from the traditional model in which everyone is funneled through a general educational system, without any clear idea of where they're going. The general education system often fails to equip the entire church and those most needing equipping seldom come. Again, because there isn't clarity in what to do with the lay people after the training, the goal simply becomes more training with little practical application.

TRAIN THROUGH DELEGATION

As a missionary in Latin America, I've kicked myself several times for not developing national leadership sooner. After all, no one could lead cell ministry quite like I could. So I waited to hand over my ministry to others. As I look back, I realize my mistake. Thankfully, I had another chance to go back to the same church and begin cell ministry all over — this time with nationals in charge.

Successfully handing over the group to the new leader is an art. More than that, it's a planned strategy. Some call this strategy "benign neglect." Randall Neighbour writes, "Increasingly involve your cell leader-in-training, and no later than month six of the cycle, announce to the cell that you will be stepping aside. Give him or her the responsibility of half the people in the cell from the beginning of the cycle (the strongest half of course!)."[7] If you understand this one point, you'll be well on your way to success in cell ministry.

Cell leaders must keep their eyes open for those who will eventually take the helm and spend the majority of their time with them. They are the future of the cell group. Make sure that you are providing opportunities for them to lead.

Don't be like Moses, who tried to do everything on his own. Moses failed to delegate his responsibilities quickly and ended up with more than one million people clamoring for his attention. Because of his failure to train others, his father-in-law, Jethro, gave him a gentle rebuke: "What you are doing is not good. You and these people who come to you will only wear yourselves out. The work is too heavy for you; you cannot handle it alone" (Exodus 18:17-10). The good news is that Moses listened to his father-in-law and appointed leadership at every level. God taught Moses to develop a new generation of leaders and to trust those under him. The one word that describes what Jethro told Moses to do is decentralize, a fancy word for shared ministry. This means to quit trying to do it all yourself and get the ministry down to the people where it belongs.

The subtle tendency for each of us in cell ministry is to do it ourselves. At times it's easier, more efficient, and time saving. But Jesus found time to spend with His disciples. The training of the 12 was his chief priority. If the cell leader does everything himself, the others in the cell group will miss out on the opportunity of exercising their spiritual gifts, serving, and learning new responsibilities.

DEVELOP A TEAM

Michael Jordan is probably the greatest basketball player that ever walked the face of this earth. Jordan loves to compete in everything that he does, but more importantly, he likes to win. Early in his career Jordan relied heavily on his own personal talent and efforts to win games. Yet, as he matured he focused on leading a team of winners. It paid off and the Chicago Bulls won the national championship year after year.

Team leadership in the context of a group has played an important role throughout the Bible. It was never God's primary will to appoint one king to rule over His people Israel. He longed for a shared leadership among prophets, judges, and elders. The people, however, cried out for a king (1 Samuel 8:4-9).

Cell members often cry out for a king. They want one person to rule. It's the cell leader's job, however, to gently remind the group that everyone is a potential leader and that everyone must actively participate.

The best way to do this is for cell leaders to ask faithful members to participate in team leadership. Cell members (potential leaders) learn best when cell ministry is modeled for them in a group setting, and team leadership provides that modeling. When a future leader can first participate in a team setting, he or she breaks the fear barrier and is more willing to assume future responsibility for the group.

When a team, instead of an individual, leads a cell group one person does not dominate the entire meeting. God gives ministry abilities to people in a variety of ways and team ministry helps us remember that no one is complete in himself or herself. One team member plans the icebreaker, another leads the worship, one leads the lesson, and another directs the prayer time. How refreshing it is to receive ministry from a wide variety of personalities and giftings.

Sadly, many leaders prefer to do it all by themselves. This problem might stem from insecurity, lack of time, or just plain ignorance. Leaders often fail by not working with and through others in order to accomplish goals in a collaborative manner.

One cell church I visited won't even multiply a "team-less" cell. All leadership training takes place in the team. The leadership team at this church is the seedbed where new leadership is developed and raised up. From the team, the new leaders (missionaries) take responsibility for the new group.

Bill Donahue of Willow Creek Community Church believes in training new leaders in a team setting through "turbo groups" comprised entirely of apprentices. They last about six months, after which time each apprentice gives birth to a group.[8] The beauty of turbo groups is that potential leaders experience small group life as they receive on the job training in the group. Pastor Doug Banister, of the Fellowship Evangelical Free Church, heard of the idea of creating a turbo group, in which a number of potential lay leaders could be trained together. He soon gathered 12 potential leaders who agreed to meet with him for three months in a simulated cell group. Eight of the 12 went on to start small groups.[9]

Some cell churches view every cell member as a potential cell leader (every cell group is a turbo group). With this in mind, the mother cell leader actively involves each cell member in the life of the cell, knowing that he or she will eventually be leading a cell group. When a new cell leader launches a cell, the mother cell leader continues discipling the new cell leader.

WATCH THE TITLES

A title doesn't make a leader — a leader makes a leader. Stanley Huffty said, "It's not the position that makes the leader; it's the leader that makes the position." The deadening effect of placing titles on your cell members, while never allowing them to actually lead, is well documented. If you've given your potential leader the title of intern, make sure he or she is actively "interning." Margaret Thatcher, former Prime Minister once said, "Being in power is like being a lady. If you have to tell people you are, you aren't."

Titles have the power to motivate a potential cell leader into action or to place them permanently on the sidelines. Glen Martin and Gary McIntosh point out:

Some small group ministries use the term co-leader or assistant leader but this has a negative impact on the multiplication and growth of the ministry in the long run. The problem is associated with the implication that a person can be a co-leader or assistant leader forever . . . While some may think the terminology doesn't matter, if you are serious about multiplying small groups in the future, the term apprentice is the best one to use.[10]

Martin and McIntosh prefer using the term "apprentice" to describe the developing cell leader. Many use the word "intern," but even this commonly used word can suggest a long-term relationship. Why not call the person a cell leader? I agree with Randall Neighbour's words:

If your pastor or supervisor uses the term "intern" exclusively, your fledgling leaders begin to believe that internship is a long-term position in itself! The vision of your church is to raise up leaders, not a bunch of weenies who think they're supposed to watch instead of do. Call them "cell leaders" and they will become cell leaders. Call them "intern," and they will remain pew warmers.[11]

I agree with Randall's advice. I personally don't use titles such as assistant or intern for potential cell leaders. Rather, I tell all members in my cell group that each one of them will eventually be leading a cell group. Some will be closer to actually leading than others, depending on where he or she is in the equipping process.

Granted, not everyone is ready to reach that high and call each person a potential cell leader. At the very least, each member should be encouraged to form part of the leadership team. The members should know that the cell leader is not the only leader in the cell group. Team ministry means others are on their way up and might soon be replacing the cell leader.

RELEASE FACILITATORS AS OPPOSED TO BIBLE TEACHERS

Many misconceptions abound about cell leadership. The idea is still prevalent that cell groups and Bible studies are the same thing. For many, therefore, cell leaders are Bible teachers. Perhaps in a bygone era this was true, but not today. Cell leaders are enablers. They don't necessarily have the gift of teacher, prophet, or evangelist. Few leaders, in fact, are qualified to teach formally. Facilitators share their lives with transparency with those in their groups, praying always that Christ will be formed in a new way within each life.

Perhaps there would be more willingness to release leaders if we would remember the facilitation role of the cell leader. A facilitator's job description focuses on guiding the communication process, praying for cell members, calling, visitation, and reaching the lost for Christ. Facilitators are trained people who guide the discussions, encourage others, and grow with the rest of the group. The words of Barbara Fleischer capture with clarity the role of facilitator:

> The word "leader" in our common usage often implies a person who stands apart from a group and directs it. A "facilitator," on the other hand, is a servant of the group, a person there to help the group achieve its purpose . . . The facilitator, likewise, is a co-participant with others in the group, sharing personal reflections and experiences and modeling what membership in the group means. Rather than being over the group, the facilitator encourages each member to share in the responsibility for maintaining a healthy and growthful group life.[12]

THE DIFFERENCE BETWEEN TEACHING
AND FACILITATING[13]

TEACHING	FACILITATING
• Provides Information • "Fan" Communication, back and forth between teacher and students • Points out logical conclusions • Written or oral testing of memorized information	• Provides an Experience • "Circle" Communication, often only observed by Facilitator • Conclusions are discovered • Feedback — observed change in values of the disciples

Because cell ministry focuses on raising up facilitators as opposed to Bible teachers, I do not believe that it is essential that a potential leader be required to know large amounts of biblical doctrine, be a gifted teacher, or even a recognized leader in the church in order to lead a cell group. If a person has demonstrated his or her love for Jesus Christ and if that person is walking in holiness, cell leadership is a distinct possibility.

TRAINING TECHNIQUES

Personal discipleship from within is very important in the cell church. But it's not the only training technique. Some cell churches utilize classroom training, retreats, and education by extension. Notice the various techniques of leadership training:[14]

- One-on-one — personalized training in which the leader meets individually with potential leaders
- Class — multiple classroom sessions
- Pilot (turbo) group — to train an initial leadership group. Each member will eventually start his or her own group

- Retreat — one to three days in which an intensive seminar takes place (normally in a non-church setting)
- Apprentice leader — future leader learns while attending the group
- Self-study tutorial — future leader learns at his or her own pace
- Professional training — Small-group seminar or with small-group consultant

Be flexible with regard to techniques and methodology. The "right way" is the one that trains numerous, quality leaders. Remember that it shouldn't be a complicated process. The secret, in fact, is to keep it as simple and doable as possible. Avoid the danger of amassing endless leadership requirements — often for the purpose of easing your own conscience.

THE LOCATION OF THE TRAINING

Where should the training take place? In a classroom? A home? The sanctuary? Some believe that the bulk of cell leadership should take place exclusively in the cell as opposed to the classroom.[15] And truly, the cell group is under-utilized in the cell church today. Some, like Bethany World Prayer Center, the International Charismatic Mission, and Faith Community Baptist, utilize the classroom to train potential leaders.[16] I've seen training in cell churches take place in parks, streets, or homes — anyplace that's available.

At the Republic Church where I minister, we use this cliché for our training track: one training track, many methods to teach it. Everyone who enters our church must go through the same equipping track, but the equipping track can be taught one-on-one, after the normal cell meeting, or in a classroom on Sunday morning or another night during the week. The pastor of each network of cells maintains the quality control and reports to the pastoral team.

My advice is to provide many options to utilize your *one* equipping track. Give those who are teaching your equipping track the liberty to use both the cell and the classroom to train future leaders.

USE RETREATS WITHIN YOUR LEADERSHIP TRAINING

Training through the retreat setting is the newest wave of cell training. The International Charismatic Mission and Faith Community Baptist Church initiated retreat training independently of each other but now share ideas. When Ralph Neighbour, Jr. and I visited a spiritual retreat at ICM, we realized how similar it was to retreats at FCBC. Bethany World Prayer Center has now added two retreats to its training and more are following suit. What makes the retreat setting so attractive? I've noted five reasons:

- ☑ Retreats provide a powerful spiritual atmosphere that is conducive to shaping new leaders and discipling new converts.
- ☑ Retreats save time.
- ☑ It's easier for trainees to commit themselves to a concentrated period of time.
- ☑ It's easier for trainers to teach in a concentrated period instead of a longer time commitment.[17]
- ☑ It provides doable cell leader training within the context of the cell church system.

PROVIDE ONGOING LEADERSHIP CARE AND TRAINING

Most cell churches around the world offer some type of continual care and training. Woe to the church that winds the leaders up and releases them for ministry, without ever checking on their progress.[18] My first cell ministry in Quito, Ecuador started at the tail end of one of these disasters. Someone on the pastoral team recommended the need for cell ministry. "Yes, that's what we need," the rest of the team agreed. The team chose key laypersons, gave them a pep talk, and let them fly. They didn't fly very high or for very long. Discouragement set in and the vision shriveled. When Celyce and I arrived in Ecuador in 1990, the cell ministry was practically non-existent. Floyd Schwanz writes, "In order for a bird to fly, it needs to have two wings. That's also true for a small group ministry, and the two wings are permission and supervision."[19]

Hold Regular Leadership Summits

Spirit-led cell churches constantly receive new insight and directions as new challenges and needs arise constantly. Top leadership needs a forum to communicate those ideas to the cell leaders. Many cell churches require a regular summit of all cell leadership.

Don't expect too much from this summit. It shouldn't replace your cell leadership training system. It's simply a way to offer ongoing care and direction to your leaders. It is a time to communicate vision and emphasize a particular theme in the cell church (e.g. evangelism, visitation, prayer). Like BWPC, you might want to distribute your cell lessons during the monthly summit.

Normally, cell churches require that cell leaders meet with top leadership on a regular basis. How regular is regular? The range is normally from weekly meetings to monthly meetings.[20] Don't ask your cell leaders to meet weekly unless you're willing to enforce it. If the "influential" cell leaders rarely attend, their example will affect the rest. I feel that it's much better to have a monthly summit when all cell leadership is present rather than a weekly one that is sparsely attended. At the Republic Church, we hold quarterly cell leadership summits. Discover what works best for you.

Recognize Your Cell Leaders

The home group leaders should be the "heroes" of your church. They deserve special attention. After all, in the cell church, they do the evangelism, discipleship, leadership training, pastoral care, counseling, and visitation. And the vast majority of cell leaders work a separate fulltime job. Begin to reward your cell leaders with recognition and perks. Ways of recognizing them include leadership retreats, special nametags or attractive sweatshirts or T-shirts. Keep the support system that undergirds them strong and improving.

Cho, in my opinion, is the model for how to recognize cell leaders. Each cell leader at YFGC is given a carrying case that bears the emblem of the church and cell ministry. This gift demonstrates the position and importance of the cell leader. Cho regularly gives certificates as a means of recognizing special achievements among his cell leaders.[21]

The Bible tells us to recognize our leaders. Paul tells the Thessalonians: ". . . to respect those who work hard among you" (1 Th. 5:12). The New American Standard version translates this verse: ". . . appreciate those who diligently labor among you." Actually, the Greek word literally means "to perceive" or "to know" those who labor among you. Recognition basically means giving credit where credit is due. The purpose of recognition is to honor and affirm the leaders' ministries. It's akin to a "payment" for well-rendered service.

Many churches dedicate their home group leaders in front of the entire Sunday morning celebration service. At the Republic Church, we recognize our cell leaders during the Sunday morning worship service. But the paramount event to honor "those who work hard among us" is our annual cell leader dinner. Nothing is spared in order to make this dinner a memorable, first-class event.

Evaluate Your Cell Leaders

How well are you training your leadership? This question is hard to answer without concrete data. Successful restaurants or food chains, for example, post suggestion boxes at counters or exits. Customers are encouraged to give their opinions. Rarely is this the case in the church. But how will you know how well you are training without feedback from the cell leaders themselves? There are several methods for collecting this valuable data:[22]

1. Informal verbal feedback — casually talking to the leaders
2. Formal verbal feedback — formal interviews with group leaders
3. Written feedback — questionnaires
4. Instant feedback — spontaneous evaluation comments during training sessions

LOOKING AHEAD

Some training models work better than others. The successful ones are clear, doable, and fit impeccably within the cell structure. The ineffective ones rely on general education and often lose the potential leader in the maze of requirements. The following are essential for every cell church:

- A clear, doable training program for potential cell leaders.
- A Jethro system in which every leader is pastored.
- On-going training for cell leadership.[23]
- An intentional way for emerging leaders to be spotted, encouraged, and integrated into the leadership structure.

11

MODELS OF
CELL LEADER TRAINING

Not long ago, I had to explain to my daughters what a typewriter looked like. They had never seen one. My children were born in the computer age, in which we talk about living a web lifestyle. According to experts, even the computer age in which we currently live will soon be obsolete. In order for companies or institutions to survive, they must learn to live in the future and to perceive the next step with accuracy. For this reason, successful organizations invest heavily in the future.

The same pattern is true of the world-class cell churches. These churches know that their long-term success depends upon living in the future. They realize that tomorrow's leaders are today's children, adolescents, and teenagers. They invest heavily in developing and training new leadership.

Many churches, on the other hand, fail in this area. After all, there are so many *present* pressures. It seems absurd to think beyond the now. Cell churches are not immune to this type of thinking. It's even possible for a church to initiate a cell ministry and to immediately produce hundreds of cell groups. Further probing, however, often reveals that the initial growth was simply a changing of the guard. Established leaders that at one time maintained the cherished programs were relocated to lead cell groups. But without an established equipping system to produce new leadership, the leadership pool dries up, bringing the cell ministry to a screeching halt.

Strong cell churches, in contrast, develop training systems that carry the new Christian from the initial discipleship stage to leading a small group. Because the top leadership realizes that training new leaders is the chief task, the entire church functions as a leadership production system.

Writing down in detail the training system of a particular cell church is risky business. Cell churches on the cutting edge are constantly adapting and improving their training. For example, I've been studying Bethany World Prayer Center for the last four years. In that time period, BWPC has made at least four major adjustments in their training. Therefore, we can't immortalize these training systems. My hope is that you'll understand the principles behind the training tracks in these churches and then be able to apply those principles to your own situation.

THE CELL MODEL OF TRAINING

I've coined the title "The Cell Model of Leadership Training" because some, if not most, of the training in this system takes place within the cell. Admittedly, retreats, seminars, and classroom instruction are used in this model, but the training starts and flows from the cell group.

Ralph Neighbour's Emphasis

Ralph Neighbour has done more than anyone to connect new believer emergence and development with cell group ministry. Many cell churches are either using his material or have adapted it in their own context. Dr. Neighbour is the founder of TOUCH Outreach Ministries and TOUCH Publications, which now promotes his material.[1] These training guides take the new believer from rethinking his value system to learning to penetrate his own "*oikos*" (friends, neighbors, and family), with the idea of ultimately leading a small group.

Training Linked with Cell Life

The main characteristic that separates Neighbour's training manuals from most discipleship booklets (i.e. Navigator or Campus Crusade) is that they are so intimately linked with the cell group. In the cornerstone booklet, *The Arrival Kit*, Week One, Day One informs the new believer, "Your Cell Group will be served in a special way. Some day, when you have matured, you may also shepherd others as a Cell Leader. There will never be more than fifteen in your family cell, and you will soon discover that each member is on a spiritual journey with you."[2] Not only does Neighbour introduce new believer training and cell group involvement simultaneously, he also plants the seed of small group leadership.

Most material is foundational Biblical teaching designed to disciple new believers.[3] Neighbour, however, takes biblical teachings and gives them new meaning in the light of the cell group. Take, for example, the biblical teaching on fellowship. A quote out of the booklet, *Welcome To Your Changed Life*, says:

> There's an event unbelievers look forward to, often called the 'Happy Hour.' It's a time when friends get together for an hour or so and drink alcoholic spirits to 'get happy.' Perhaps you have shared in such events? Christians have the only TRUE 'Happy Hour!' It's a special time, called a 'Cell Group,' when they get together to be with their Lord.[4]

When talking about baptism, he urges the new Christian to talk with his or her cell leader as soon as possible.[5] When touching the Lord's Supper, he says, "In your *oikos*, you will observe a special meal called 'The Lord's Supper.'"[6]

Retreats supplement the cell training, and there is even a place for classroom instruction, but all training ties into the life of the cell group. Notice the relationship between Neighbour's training material and the cell:

☑ Unbeliever makes decision for Christ and is given *Welcome to Your Changed Life* and *Scripture Pack*.

☑ Cell leader or member contacts convert and gives the *Journey Guide*. At this time, the cell leader appoints a sponsor and schedules a visit.

☑ Cell leader and sponsor visit and set the "year of equipping" schedule. The sponsor then sets dates for the first session.

☑ Sponsor and disciple spend five weeks using *New Believer's Station.*

☑ Sponsor and disciple spend 11 weeks using *The Arrival Kit.* Afterwards, the disciple is encouraged to become a sponsor and begins helping new cell group members.

Sponsorship

The most unique, workable contribution of Dr. Neighbour to new believer training is the concept of sponsorship within the cell group. Sponsorship is much like one-on-one discipleship. Each new believer in the cell group is assigned a sponsor (cell member or cell leader). With the help of the sponsor, the new believer passes through the various levels of training called "stations." Neighbour writes, "Assign each new believer to someone in the group who will help them become established in their walk with Christ."[7]

The sponsor-disciple relationship lasts from three to four months. Then the relationship changes to partnership. It's during this transitional time that the sponsor trains his disciple to become a sponsor of others.[8] The sponsor focuses on the six leadership characteristics, which include listening, interceding, modeling, teaching, leading and involving the disciples with other Christians.[9]

The sponsor spends the first five weeks using the *New Believer's Station* booklet, which talks about the devotional life, freedom in Christ, and spiritual growth.[10] After covering the material in this five-week booklet, the sponsor takes the person to a Spiritual Formation Weekend retreat. The new disciple is then ready for water baptism. Next, the sponsor and the disciple spend 11 weeks in *The Arrival Kit.* Afterwards, the disciple is encouraged to become a sponsor and begins helping new cell group members. The sponsor then takes the disciple to the Spiritual Warfare Weekend and to equipping training for outreach evangelism.

Importance of Weekend Events

Neighbour believes that equipping in the cell church is most effective when it is launched in weekend events. These "weekends" are like stations on a railway system. You must first go to a station before beginning a journey. At these stations, there is intensive orientation to prepare you for the next stage of the journey. Each weekend launches a study, a ministry, or an activity. Further training and practical experience is tied to each weekend. For example, the Spiritual Formation Weekend launches the study of *The New Believer's Station*; the Touching Hearts Weekend is followed by the *Touching Hearts Guidebook*, etc.

Weekend events are intimately tied to the cell group. Enlistment for the weekends, for example, takes place in the cell group meeting; the cell leader gives approval to take the training, registering cell members with a card. The cell leader also asks those who have been trained to share what they learned at the next cell meeting. In the case of the Touching Hearts Weekend, a team of two returns to the cell group and shares the presentation with the entire group during the next two meetings.

Training for Outreach

Neighbour believes that the most effective outreach reaches friends, neighbors, and family members, which he labels our *oikos*.[11] Training for outreach takes place in special training weekends. The order is as follows:

- Cell leader sends team to Touching Hearts Weekend — church-wide training for harvesting Type A unbelievers. Participants work through the *Touching Hearts Guidebook*.
- Cell leader sends team to interest group training — church-wide training for harvesting Type B unbelievers. Teams work through the *Opening Hearts Trilogy*.

Neighbour distinguishes between "Type A" unbelievers who are familiar with religious customs and "Type B" unbelievers who ". . . are not searching for Jesus Christ, and show no interest in Bible study or other Christian activities."[12]

For the "Type B" unbelievers, Dr. Neighbour has designed a "non-Christian type" cell group called Share Groups. These Share Groups do not replace the normal cell groups but serve as an extension of an outreach from the regular cell group. Those believers who start or participate in Share Groups have the dual responsibility of attending their normal cell groups as well as separate Share Groups.

Share Groups are short-term, normally lasting ten weeks.[13] They move from house to house, and the goal is to bring the converts and seekers to the Shepherd Group. Concerning these Share Groups Neighbour says, "This group should be free, informal, and spontaneous . . . It's important for all Share Group members to feel they can be themselves."[14] He goes on to say:

> Share Groups are the most Biblical and effective means for reaching the unchurched. Few will be won by evangelistic visits, evangelistic luncheons, or Bible studies. We are dealing with disillusioned, cynical, and damaged people who have already been "run over" by churches, and who are not ready for another experience with them. Sadly, for years, I have watched the pros in evangelism shy away from Share Groups because they begin with relationships rather than with Bible studies. When we refuse to meet the unchurched where they are, and demand they meet on our terms, we are hopelessly separated from each other.[15]

Target Groups are similar to Share Groups. The major difference lies in the homogeneous nature of Target Groups. Target Groups might include groups for the divorced, professionals, mothers, alcoholics, etc.

Neighbour's concept of the Share Group and Target Group resembles the cell planting emphasis in other cell churches (e.g., International Charismatic Mission, Bethany World Prayer Center). The difference is that new cell plants among interest groups in many churches are classified as regular, ongoing cell groups. In contrast, the Share Groups and Target Groups designed by Ralph Neighbour are sub-cells and never categorized as actual cells. They serve to funnel new converts into Shepherd cells.

Biblical Emphasis

For each stage of the spiritual development, Neighbour highlights a corresponding book or books of the Bible. Ideally each new believer will cover the Bible. This is not a required part of the training system. Rather, the following Bible books deepen the spiritual life of the believer. This chart explains the process:

NEIGHBOUR'S DISCIPLESHIP TRACK[16]

YOUR JOURNEY INTO A LIFETIME OF MINISTRY	
☑ Rethinking my value system	Pentateuch
☑ Learning to be a sponsor	History/Poetry
☑ Learning to use the John 3:16 diagram	Major Prophets/Minor Prophets
☑ Bringing "Type A" unbelievers to Christ	Gospels
☑ Being equipped for ministry and spiritual warfare	Acts
☑ Learning to conduct share/interest groups	Pauline Epistles/Regular Epistles
☑ Learning to penetrate new *oikoses*	Revelation

The 52-week self-study of the Bible includes a five-minute-per-day taped message. At six-week intervals the cell leader (or church leadership) provides a special question/answer evening for all those taking the one-year Bible course.[17]

Influence of Neighbour's Training Track

Faith Community Baptist Church, which has an enormous influence on cell churches in Asia, emulates Neighbour's training system almost entirely (I decided not to include it in this book because it was so similar to Neighbour's model). Many cell churches in the U.S., such as Long Reach Church of God (Pastor Bob Davis) and Cornerstone Church (Pastor Gerald Martin), have been strongly influenced by Neighbour's training model.

LITTLE FALLS CHRISTIAN CENTRE
LITTLE FALLS ROODEPOORT, SOUTH AFRICA
PASTOR HAROLD F. WEITSZ
FACTS: 240 CELLS; 3000 SUNDAY ATTENDANCE

Personally, I believe that the equipping track of Little Falls Christian Centre is one of best on the cell church market today. Pastor Harold Weitsz, a close friend of mine, stole with pride the best of Ralph Neighbour's equipping track and then adapted it to his own context. (See illustration at the top of the following page).

Every potential leader attends the training track consisting of four weekend encounters spread over a four-month period. That's right — a cell leader is trained in four months! Preceding each encounter weekend, each member receives a process booklet with questions to answer. After completion of this booklet, the cell leader reviews and signs it, thus permitting the member to attend the encounter weekend. The booklet becomes the "entry ticket" for the appropriate

Equipping Track Steps

Little Falls
Christian Centre
Little Falls Roodepoort, South Africa

encounter weekend and qualifies the person to receive the weekend training manual.

The four encounter weekends cover basic concepts of Christianity: spiritual freedom and victory, soul winning and cell leadership training. Each weekend is held in the church, starts on Friday night, and finishes on Saturday. The member must faithfully attend his cell meeting to fulfill the assignments of the weekend. Once the course has been completed the new leader is expected to attend the quarterly general leadership training weekend.

The weekend encounters repeat continuously throughout the year and enable each member to select four weekends suitable to his or her lifestyle and other commitments. One can therefore complete the four encounters in a four month period or longer.

After becoming a cell leader, further training takes place. There is specialized training for cell group overseers, and a two-year course of the LFCC College must be completed by all who emerge as new potential pastors from the ranks of the cell overseers.

Newly trained leaders may begin their own cells, connecting them to the current Jethro-type structure, or are even encouraged to plant new cells at the workplace or with people of similar interest (e.g. sports, hobbies or activities). This equipping track is capable of training hundreds of new cell leaders per year.

BETHANY WORLD PRAYER CENTER
BAKER, LOUISIANA
PASTOR LARRY STOCKSTILL
FACTS: 700 CELLS; 8,000 SUNDAY ATTENDANCE

Bethany World Prayer Center lives on the cutting edge of cell church ministry. BWPC continually adapts its cell leadership training in order to improve it. I have placed BWPC under the Cell Model of training new leaders because a large part of the training takes place within the cell. It's equally true, however, that BWPC uses retreats and the classroom to train potential cell leaders. Like all cell-training models, BWPC has taken principles from other models while maintaining its own creativity.

The training path at BWPC is crystal clear. The new believer immediately learns how to hit a homerun — how to go from A (new convert) to B (cell leader). The goal for everyone is the same: become a leader of a cell group. BWPC uses a baseball diamond to illustrate the process. (See illustration at the top of the following page).

It takes about eight months to get around the bases. A new believer at Bethany first enters a cell group. From there, a sponsor from the cell group (cell leader or member) guides that person through the *Christianity 101* booklet. This booklet covers the meaning of salvation, water baptism, disciplines of Christian growth, baptism of the Holy Spirit, cell group ministry, and evangelism. The new disciple is then baptized.

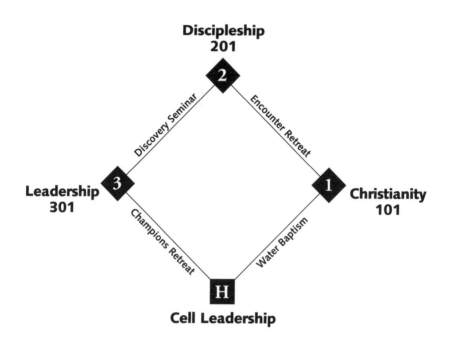

The next step is an Encounter Retreat in which new believers find help in overcoming the problems in their lives. Staff pastors help the person isolate satanic strongholds and determine spiritual needs.

When the person leaves the Encounter retreat, he or she is placed in *Discipleship 201*. This is where he or she learns to change values. The *Discipleship 201* booklet is used to teach the potential leaders basic Bible doctrine, practical tips on how to live their new life in Christ, and insight into their relationships with the local church.[18] The potential leaders are taught the importance of praying, fasting, and studying the Bible. *Discipleship 201* is taught as a 12-week class on Wednesday nights in the church.[19]

Then the potential leaders attend a Discovery Seminar, where they learn their personality styles, their spiritual gifts, and are prepared for future cell leadership.

After the Discovery Seminar, they come to third base, which is *Leadership 301*. This is a 12-lesson class that helps them to learn about cells. They are discipled in the principles of time management and leadership.

The last step is a Champion's Retreat. The potential leaders are taken to a local hotel and given a banquet and more training. On Saturday, Pastor Larry Stockstill speaks to them. Then on Sunday morning, all the new leaders are presented before the church. Friends come forward and pray for them as they are commissioned into ministry. In this way, Bethany always has a fresh supply of new leaders. They don't have to look farther than their own congregation to raise-up new leadership.

THE GROUP TRAINING MODEL

I've labeled this model the "Group Training Model" because the bulk of the training takes place in a classroom or retreat setting. In this system, very little training takes place within the cell. Rather, cell leaders ask cell members to take the training courses in the church and/or in a retreat setting that is administered and taught within each homogeneous department.

The most prominent cell church using this model is the International Charismatic Mission though other cell churches also train their leaders in a group format (e.g., Colonial Hills Baptist Church in Southaven, Mississippi). The Republic Church, where I currently serve, has adapted aspects of this model.

INTERNATIONAL CHARISMATIC MISSION
BOGOTA, COLOMBIA
PASTOR CÉSAR CASTELLANOS
FACTS: 20,000 CELLS; 45,000 SUNDAY ATTENDANCE

ICM does not use one-on-one training in the cell. New believers are trained in a class setting along with many others. The training at ICM takes approximately six months to complete. Although this is the average time, some homogeneous departments at ICM take less time, and others more. The following steps outline the official process for every new convert. However, some new converts don't attend an Encounter Retreat immediately. Instead, they enter the School of Leadership and only later attend an Encounter Retreat. Flexibility, therefore, is possible within ICM's training.

Steps One & Two: Initial Follow-up and Life in the Cell

During the celebration services (entire church on Sunday) or congregational service (one of the homogeneous group gatherings), there is always the opportunity to receive Jesus Christ. Large numbers respond and are gathered into a separate room after the service. Trained workers present the gospel once again in a more personal manner.

The information of each new convert is placed on cards, which are immediately entered into the computer system at ICM. This information is distributed to the different homogeneous departments, and within 48 hours cell leaders contact the new believers.

The new person begins the Christian life in a cell group. The new convert receives personal care and spiritual food within the group. In the context of the cell group, each person is pastored — but not trained. This is one of the key differences in the Group Training Model.

Within the cell group, the new convert will hear about a three day retreat called an Encounter Retreat. Before attending this event, the new convert must take three preparatory lessons taught in a classroom setting.

Step Three: Pre-Encounter

Before attending an Encounter Retreat new believers are required to complete three of six Navigators books on the basics of Christian life. The purpose for this step is to give each person a few biblical foundations before arriving at an Encounter Retreat. Each lesson is offered in a classroom setting in the church by a trained teacher within the particular homogeneous group (one lesson per week).

Step Four: Encounter Retreat

Those who receive Jesus Christ as adults are often bound up by past hurts, dysfunctional behavior, and sinful patterns. The act of "accepting Jesus" saves them from eternal hell, but doesn't instantly change their behavior. The Encounter Retreat is a three-day event designed to help liberate the new believer from past bondage. ICM believes that a three-day Encounter Retreat is equal to one whole year of attending the church.[20]

An Encounter Retreat begins on Friday evening and finishes late Sunday afternoon. Between 70-120 people attend a retreat held away from the city and routine schedules in order to concentrate fully on God.

The Encounter Retreat deals with four areas in the person's life. First, there is teaching on the *security of salvation*. Second, the participants experience *liberation and inner healing*. Designated leaders teach the people the true meaning of repentance and how to live in broken surrender before God. Third, the Encounter Retreat is a time to receive the *fullness of the Spirit of God*. Fourth, the new believer receives teaching about the *vision of ICM*.[21] Those attending hear ICM's plans to use each one of them in cell ministry.

Step Five: Post-Encounter

The Post-Encounter takes place immediately after the Encounter Retreat and prepares the new believer to enter the School of Leaders. The final three Navigator lessons are offered during this time, and again, these lessons are taught in a group setting (mostly in a classroom).

Step Six: School of Leadership

After the Post-Encounter teaching, the young believer begins attending the yearlong School of Leadership. This consists of a two-hour weekly class that takes place among the different homogeneous groups.

César Castellanos has written a book for each semester. *Encounter One* (first semester) covers God's purpose for mankind, man's sinful condition, the person of Jesus Christ, and the uniqueness of Christianity. *Encounter Two* (second semester) deals with the cross of Jesus Christ. *Encounter Three* (third semester) teaches baptism, the devotional life, authority of the Scriptures, and the doctrine of the Holy Spirit.[22] Another manual, *C.A.F.E. 2000* (a compilation of cell leadership training material), is taught alongside the Encounter manuals in order to prepare the person to lead a cell group.

Step Seven: Second Encounter Retreat

This second retreat is designed to reinforce the commitments made at the first retreat and to instill final principles in the potential leader before he or she launches a cell group.[23] The second retreat normally occurs after the first semester of the School of Leadership, immediately before the person starts leading his or her cell group.

Step Eight: Lead a Cell Group

It's important to remember that a person doesn't have to finish the entire School of Leadership before opening a cell group. Many, in fact, lead an open cell before attending a second Encounter Retreat. Often, the School of Leadership provides ongoing training for those already leading a cell group.

Step Nine: More in-depth Teaching

For those cell leaders who desire more advanced training, there is a graduate level training track that uses a series of materials entitled "Firm as a Rock."

Step Ten: School of Teachers

The School of Teachers is a course designed to train potential teachers to teach in the School of Leadership. Potential teachers are taught various teaching skills and especially how to apply the teaching to the lives of their students.

TWO EXAMPLES OF CELL CHURCHES INFLUENCED BY ICM

After visiting the International Charismatic Mission, my senior pastor, Pastor Porfirio Ludeña, guided us to change our equipping track to the Group Training Model. Previously, our training began with one-on-one discipleship.[24] Now new trainees must be involved in a cell, but we also offer training in classes, just like ICM does. Although we still grant the liberty to teach the equipping track in a one-on-one setting, most new believers receive training in a group setting (our motto is to maintain one training track but use various methods to teach it).

Another example is Pastor Rakjumar Patta of King's Temple in Hyderabad, Central India, who tried implementing the cell church philosophy for several years, without success. The 15 groups they had at one stage dwindled to only two. When they heard what was happening at the International Charismatic Mission, they decided to transition their church to that model. They told everyone that they would eventually be leading a group, and that everyone would reach this goal at his/her own speed. Instead of looking for one intern in the group to be trained to lead the next group, each cell leader began seeing all group members as potential leaders. The church also decided that all training and teaching would be done by a strong central leadership team, and not by the individual cell group leaders. In taking the burden from the cell leader, this church hoped that it would release many more people from the fear of leading a group. After implementing these changes, the church experienced spectacular growth.[25]

THE GROUP TRAINING MODEL AT COLONIAL HILLS BAPTIST CHURCH
SOUTHAVEN, MISSISSIPPI
PASTOR STEVE BENNETT

The equipping track at Colonial Hills Baptist Church has evolved since 1995. Initially, they emphasized one-on-one discipleship, but found it very difficult, even with partnership accountability, to motivate people to go through the entire equipping track (about 10 months in length). They tried several adaptations and modifications until they eventually scrapped the whole process and adopted a Saddleback model of the Four Bases.

Now they incorporate the equipping track material into four, four-hour presentations (16 hours total) with more to follow. The training begins at 8 o'clock on a Saturday morning in the church and ends at noon. For five dollars they provide a good breakfast (7:30 a.m.), childcare, and a syllabus with the materials to be covered. Senior staff members lead the bases and they use a classroom/church setting. The church also does specific training for leaders in retreat settings (cell leaders, interns, supervisors, etc.).

First base is taught by the senior pastor. It deals with the history, vision, philosophy, and future of the church. All church members are encouraged to attend, as are prospective members interested in the church. Second base deals with personal soul care. The associate pastor and a couple of zone pastors teach it. Things such as salvation, how to study the Bible, tithing and giving, and praying are dealt with. Third base deals with who the individual is in Christ. It is taught by the minister of worship, the youth pastor, and a zone pastor. Spiritual gifts, personality, experiences, abilities, and heart, are covered to help one find his spiritual shape. Fourth base deals with one's place in the ministry of CHBC. It is taught by zone pastors and the children's minister.

THE HUDDLE MODEL OF TRAINING

I'm not sure where the word "Huddle" originated, but it describes the purpose of a weekly meeting. Floyd L. Schwanz, formally a pastor at New Hope Community Church in Portland, Oregon, describes the huddle in this way:

> Several years ago two pastors were in my office to talk about small-group ministries. They were very concerned about how much training these leaders had received. I told them they had completed a weekend of training. And when they asked (with emphasis), "That's it?" I told them that they also came to weekly training as long as they wanted to be in leadership . . . One of them wrinkled up his face and asked, "You have to go

to that every week?" Obviously, he was thinking with a mind-set that this was a leaders' class. No, not at all. This is a huddle. Remember as a pastor I serve as a coach, and these leaders form my team.[26]

Various small group churches depend on weekly leadership training meetings to equip their cell leaders. The churches listed under the "Huddle Model" also train their leaders in seminars, classrooms, and use an effective Jethro structure. The crown jewel, however, is the ongoing, weekly training — the Huddle.[27] This continual training fulfills such an important role in these churches that potential leaders are given only minimal pre-training before leading a cell group. These churches depend on the unending sessions to give the new leaders fresh vision, specific training, and whatever help is necessary.

THE META MODEL

The Meta Model relies on frequent Huddles to maintain leadership quality. The Meta Model is a contextualized model of small group ministry for the North American church, which was popularized by Carl George and originally patterned after the small group ministry at the New Hope Community Church in Portland Oregon.[28] Apart from the pure cell churches that I examined, I have also observed various churches that use the Meta Model — Willow Creek Community Church, Saddleback Community Church, Cincinnati Vineyard, and Fairhaven Alliance Church.[29]

Less Up-Front Training

The Meta Model requires less up-front training. George, the philosophical thinker behind the Meta Model, sets forth his reasoning in *The Coming Church Revolution*:

Those who plan training and leadership development in churches tend to overdo orientation training and under do supervision. Why? Their own educational upbringing has made them comfortable with orientation training but relatively unfamiliar with the notion of supervision . . . any growing Christian . . . will be able to put together lots of the pieces on a common-sense basis with only a small amount of instruction.[30]

More Ongoing Training

To compensate for the lack of up-front training, each cell leader and intern in the Meta Model must attend on-going bimonthly leadership training.[31] Ideally, they are required to meet every other week in a general leadership-training event called the VHS (Vision, Huddle, and Skill Training). In *Prepare Your Church for the Future*, George dedicates 30 pages to describe how the ongoing leadership training meetings works with the Jethro structure to train and care for cell leadership.[32]

In all of the Meta Models there is some type of ongoing leadership training, but this system seems to be very flexible. Willow Creek gathers its leadership community every month for training and encouragement.[33] Saddleback Community Church, on the other hand, requires quarterly training meetings.[34]

THE ELIM CHURCH
SAN SALVADOR, EL SALVADOR
PASTOR MARIO VEGA
FACTS: 5500 CELLS; 35,000 SUNDAY ATTENDANCE

The Elim Church depends heavily on the weekly Huddle to provide ongoing care and training. Leadership training is very basic. There are very few initial requirements. This is partly due to the ongoing care that each cell leader receives.

The Huddle takes place on the zone level instead of the church level because of the massive size of the cell ministry. Zone pastors meet weekly with supervisors and cell leaders to teach the weekly lesson, so that they in turn can teach it to their groups. EC prepares the lessons in written form for the cell leader and then diligently trains the leader on lesson delivery. Little is left for chance. Encouragement, motivation, and vision are transmitted during these meetings. All cell leaders are required to attend the weekly Huddle.

A four-week training course is a prerequisite to cell leadership. Normally, the district pastor teaches this course, with the help of a zone pastor. Each district offers this course repeatedly throughout the year. The following table explains the content of this leadership-training course:

EC — NEW LEADER TRAINING COURSE

FIRST WEEK	The Calling to Lead
	The Vision of the Cell Group
	The Reason for Cell Groups
SECOND WEEK	Requirements and Characteristics of Leadership
	Lesson Preparation
THIRD WEEK	How the Cell Groups Operate
	How the Cell Groups Multiply
FOURTH WEEK	Administration and Organization of Cell Groups
	Final Exam

The mid-week expository Bible teaching service is designed to provide foundational Bible training, but the weekly Huddle provides the ongoing supervision and training.[35]

FOLLOW THE PRINCIPLES

Don't follow methods; rather, extract principles from the methods and apply them to your situation. We've seen how cell churches that are serious about reaping the harvest invest heavily in future leadership. We've looked at their equipping systems for developing small group leaders for the harvest. Yet we must now go beyond their models and look closely at the principles.

12

THE PRINCIPLES
BEHIND THE MODELS

English dog trainer Barbara Woodhouse says, "I can train any dog in five minutes. It's training the owners that takes longer."[1] If Woodhouse were a cell church consultant, I could hear her say, "I can train a new cell leader in less than six months. It's training the church that takes longer." Sporadic training of individual leaders is common in many churches. Few churches, however, establish a systematic training system that produces large numbers of small group leaders.

Warning: Most churches pass through multiple revisions of their equipping track before finding the right fit. Initial failure often occurs because a church tries to copy another church's training model in its entirety. Most often the church realizes that the training model doesn't fit its unique context and identity. To help you avoid this landmine, I've extracted seven principles from the best cell church training models. These principles should undergird your equipping track, although the form of your model will be distinct.

PRINCIPLE #1:
KEEP THE TRAINING TRACK SIMPLE

Don't over-complicate your cell leadership training track. In the early days, the International Charismatic Mission developed a two-year equipping track for cell leaders that included homiletics, theology 1,2,3, etc. By the time a person graduated from that equipping track he or she had lost contact with non-Christian friends. I recommend using only four manuals or having only four steps. Most cell church equipping tracks prepare their leaders in the following four areas:

- Basic doctrine
- Inner-life Development
- Personal evangelism
- Leadership training

The first area or step is basic Bible doctrine. All evangelical Christians would agree that the teaching of God's Word is the foundation of the new believer's life. Does this mean that the new believer must take systematic theology 1,2,3,4 that takes four years to complete? Definitely not. I studied systematic theology in Bible college and seminary, but as a new believer I needed the milk of God's Word — the basic principles.

One seminar attendee asked me, "What kind of Bible doctrine should I cover in my training track?" I told him that it was important to include basic teaching about God, sin, the person of Jesus Christ, salvation, the Holy Spirit, and the church. I also told him that he must decide if this initial course would include six, nine, or fourteen lessons. The number of lessons in the first manual will depend on how much biblical doctrine your church deems necessary for the new believer.

The second area, inner-life development, focuses on devotional life. The goal is to help new believers feed themselves. This step is summed up in the saying, "Give a man a fish and you feed him for a day; teach him how to fish and you feed him for a lifetime." The first step provides an understanding of basic biblical teaching while the second step helps the new believer nourish himself from God's Word. The teaching of this stage should also deal with confession of sin, forgiveness, and steps to freedom from past bondages. Christ wants to heal every sin and scar of the past, and the manual for this step should cover these issues. New believers should learn that they have direct access to the throne of God because of the blood of Jesus.

The third area, personal evangelism, teaches the person how to share his or her faith. Each believer needs to learn how to lead someone else to Jesus Christ. This stage teaches the plan of salvation in a systematic, step-by-step process. Beyond learning the content of the gospel presentation, the believer must also learn how to develop friendships with non-Christians (i.e., reaching his personal contacts-*oikos*). The effectiveness of small group evangelism is also highlighted, and teaching is given on how the cell functions like a team to evangelize non-Christians as well as providing the ideal atmosphere for non-believers.

The final area covers how to lead a cell group. The manual for this stage should cover the basics of cell ministry, small group dynamics (e.g., how to listen well, transparent sharing, etc.), how to lead a cell group, and characteristics of godly leaders. I like to teach this manual in a home setting to provide a small group feeling and give the group opportunity to practice small group dynamics. This manual should include teaching about the ideal order of a cell meeting (Welcome, Worship, Word , and Works).

PRINCIPLE #2:
PROVIDE ACTION STEPS WITH THE TRAINING

Make sure that your training is practical, and that you have an action
step for each step of your training. I've included four basic action steps
that could be included in a four-step equipping track.

- ☑ First step: Basic Doctrine
  Include the action step of baptism in water
- ☑ Second Step: Inner Development
  Include the action step of having a regular devotional time
- ☑ Personal Evangelism
  Include the action step of witnessing and inviting a non-
  Christian to the cell group
- ☑ Leadership Training
  Include the action step of leading a cell group

Beyond completing the above action steps, all those taking training
must be actively involved in a cell group. By actively, I mean leading
various activities in the cell group. If you use the four Ws (Welcome,
Worship, Word, Works), the trainee must lead each W, under the
direction of the cell leader. One month, for example, the trainee could
lead the Welcome time, another month the Worship time, etc.

PRINCIPLE #3: PREPARE A SECOND LEVEL OF TRAINING
FOR CELL LEADERS

Many cell churches fall into the trap of over-complicating the first
level of training. They try to place too many steps of training in the
first level and potential cell leaders never arrive at the point of leading
a cell group.

My advice is to divide your training into at least two levels. The first level should include the four basic areas or steps (each area is normally embodied in a manual). It's important that the first level is not too complicated and allows rapid preparation of cell leaders. The second level provides additional training for cell leaders (second level training is only for those leading a cell group).

The Little Falls Christian Centre in South Africa has developed an exemplary equipping system. Their first level is clear, concise, and trains new believers rapidly to enter cell leadership. In 1999, 970 passed through this first level and were able to eliminate the cell leader shortage in their church. LFCC also has a second level of training for those who are leading a cell group. The second level provides added biblical and spiritual nourishment for those most needing it — the front-line soldiers.

The Door of Hope Church (pastor Al Woods) is another great example of second-tier training. This church has developed a leadership-training track for cell leaders and zone shepherds (overseers of 3-6 cells).

In the second level, you could add additional doctrinal courses, a spiritual warfare course, teaching on spiritual gifts, etc. There is considerable room for creativity and many excellent courses and materials. One cell church decided to use their denomination's theological education by extension for this second level. Cell leaders deserve special treatment because of their important, foundational role in the church. My advice is to treat them like royalty. Offer them all the help and training that they need in order to be effective.

Some cell churches even offer a third and fourth level of training, leading to pastoral ministry. Faith Community Baptist Church features an extensive training program to prepare higher-level leaders (i.e., zone pastors). Bethany World Prayer Center hosts a three-year Bible school on their own property. Neither church requires higher education for cell leadership — it's simply provided for those who feel called to full-time ministry (and who have been successful in leading and multiplying their cell group).

PRINCIPLE #4:
USE ONLY ONE EQUIPPING TRACK

While you should allow flexibility in the training methodology (next principle), you should only have one training track. After deciding on a church-wide training track (ideally both first and second levels), a church should require that all future leaders pass through the same training. This will assure that:
- All future cell leaders are biblically and spiritually trained.
- All are prepared to evangelize and lead a cell.
- All are in-line with the leadership of the church.
- All understand the church's vision.

To guarantee long-term success, you want to make sure every future leader has passed through the same process and has received the same training.

PRINCIPLE #5: THERE IS NO ONE METHODOLOGY FOR IMPLEMENTING YOUR TRAINING

Some believe that the only way to train new believers is one-on-one. Others disagree and train new believers in a group setting. During one seminar, I mentioned that our church most commonly trains new believers in a group setting. One person shook his head in disbelief and said, "But isn't one-on-one discipleship in the cell group the only true way to equip new believers?" I reminded him that even Jesus didn't always use the one-on-one discipleship format. He trained the 12 in a group.

Don't confuse the training methodology (where or how you train people) with the training track (the steps of training.). From my study of the fastest growing cell churches around the world, I've noticed a great variety of methodologies for implementing the training model (e.g., one-on-one discipleship, one-on-two or three, training after the cell group, seminars, classes, retreats, or a combination of all of them). In the last chapter, I highlighted that both the Group Training Model and the Cell Model work effectively. Colonial Hills Baptist Church uses the group training method in the seminar format. Bethany World Prayer Center, on the other hand, starts the training within the cell using one-on-one discipleship. The training at Bethany then diversifies into a variety of settings. Don't become overly rigid on the methodology that you use.

PRINCIPLE #6:
TRAIN EVERYONE TO BECOME A CELL LEADER

Ideally, each new believer in the church should immediately start attending a cell group and begin the equipping track. In reality, it often takes more time. However, the more a church closes the gap between idealism and realism, the more effective it will be. We don't pressure those who refuse to enter our training to become cell leaders, but we're constantly promoting it (both at the cell level and at the celebration level). Those who desire to follow the vision of the church enter training to become cell leaders.

PRINCIPLE #7:
CONTINUALLY ADJUST AND IMPROVE THE TRAINING

You should be fine-tuning your equipping system continually. The Cornerstone Church, led by Pastor Gerald Martin, has been working on its model for seven years. Dennis Wadley, a pastor in Santa Barbara, CA says that their equipping track has been in a process of development for three years, as they have been creating and recreating the tools. You also will need to adapt, adjust, and improve your training system as you receive feedback from your members.

MORE THAN ONE MODEL

Rather than telling you what I think is the best model, I've offered principles that will help you form your own unique equipping system. Analyze and digest the principles in this chapter along with the models presented in chapter 11. Then spend time in God's presence as you form your own training track.

13

MATERIALS FOR TRAINING
CELL LEADERS

While living in Pasadena, California, I learned the benefits of belonging to an automobile club. Before traveling long-distances by car, I would first ask an automobile club worker to map out the best route. Within minutes I knew exactly how to get to my destination. I could then enjoy the ride because my directions were clearly written down.

I hope the previous chapters have helped you to determine where you want to go. Yet, this book wouldn't be complete without suggesting specific material to help you arrive at your destination — to allow you to enjoy the ride.

SPECIFIC MATERIAL

The best equipping tracks highlight excellent material. The materials in these equipping tracks promote the basic doctrines of the faith (along with the specific vision of the church), spiritual life development, evangelism, and leadership training. They are concise and clear and don't overwhelm the learner.

There are two major points to remember when selecting training material for your cell church. First, is it biblical? Does it reflect the pure doctrine "once delivered by the saints?" Second, is it connected with your cell church philosophy? In other words, is the training conducive to convert every member into a cell leader?

Bethany World Prayer Center has developed three booklets called *Christianity 101, Discipleship 201,* and *Leadership 301.* Notice the progression. The first covers the basics of the Christian faith — how to get started growing in Jesus. The second goes deeper and helps a believer live a victorious Christian life. The third booklet orients the believer with basic leadership skills in order to effectively lead a cell group. After leading a cell group, Bethany offers additional material (even a three-year Bible college).

Ralph Neighbour's equipping track offers a number of booklets. Neighbour has spent the major part of his years perfecting training material for every aspect of cell life — new Christian development, Bible curricula, evangelism training, gifts of the Spirit, spiritual warfare, and more.[1] The believer is told from day one that eventually he or she will be leading a cell group.

The International Charismatic Mission uses three main books written by César Castellanos called *Encounter 1, Encounter 2,* and *Encounter 3.* All three Encounter books focus on biblical doctrine, mixed in with the vision of the church. The goal is to equip church members to lead a cell group. When the student then begins leading a cell group, additional, higher-level material is available.

Little Falls Christian Centre has developed its own material. Each book leads to higher-level learning. The equipping track starts with basic doctrinal training in *Welcome to Your New Family;* then the new believer receives more in-depth discipleship in the *Arrival Kit Companion*; the *Reaching the Lost* booklet prepares the potential leader to evangelize, whereas the *Cell Leader Equipping Manual* launches him into cell leadership. A more in depth manual, taught in a retreat, accompanies each booklet. The concise material at LFCC propels the trainee to lead a cell group in just four months!

Our own material at the Republic Church possesses this same clarity. We begin with a course on basic biblical truths, which leads to a Bible panorama course. The potential leader is then thoroughly trained in evangelism. The fourth and final manual before launching the cell is called *Leadership in the Cell Church*. Of course, the trainee is exercising his spiritual muscles in the cell group while busily completing the four manuals. Although our training normally takes nine months, it is possible to complete it in six. We offer higher-level training for cell leaders — but only cell leaders. We don't continue to educate those sitting on the sidelines.

The material used in most traditional churches is endless. It is often great material, but it doesn't lead to a specific destination. Because the focus is on general education, there's no limit to what must be learned and no direction for the person being educated.

MATERIALS FROM CELL CHURCHES WORLD WIDE

Most cell churches around the world have developed their own materials. You can take advantage of their experiences. Remember the words of leadership expert Tom Peters: "The best leaders . . . are the best 'note-takers', the best 'askers,' the best learners. They are shameless thieves."[2] Peters recommends the title, "*Swiped from the Best with Pride.*"[3] Someone has said that "plagiarism" is copying one man's material while "research" is gathering the materials of many. On a more serious note, plagiarism is a sin and the law forbids us to make whole photocopies of someone else's copyrighted material. We can, however, use their ideas and synthesize them with our own.

The Clearpoint Church in Houston, Texas (Pastor Blake McKenzie) has taken the best from Saddleback Community Church, Ralph Neighbour, Bethany World Prayer Center and others that are effective at equipping believers.

Long Reach Church of God (Pastor Bob Davis) has elected to use "The Year of Equipping" by Ralph Neighbour. They have followed the basic format for the Freedom (Victory) Encounter, Spiritual Formations and the Touching Hearts Weekend.

The International Charismatic Mission borrowed extensively from another cell church in Guatemala called *Fraternidad Cristiana de Guatemala*.[4] The Christian Center in Guayaquil borrowed concepts from Neighbour, the Elim Church and the International Charismatic Mission. Little Falls Christian Centre took the best from Neighbour and then synthesized it into four booklets and manuals.[5] We've done the same in our own church. I recommend the following process:

1. Obtain Copies of Other Equipping Material

Research what is out there. Obtain copies of the material from the best cell churches, such as Bethany World Prayer Center, and other cell churches listed in this book (I've provided e-mails and phone numbers in the footnotes).[6] David Cho's teaching is now available in written form, in a five-book series.[7] TOUCH Outreach Ministries provides the excellent material developed by RalphNeighbour.

2. Test the Material

After receiving materials from a variety of sources, review and test them to determine those that best fit your church. Some material works better in more educated churches, while others are designed to equip those with less schooling. You will also want to evaluate the stance taken on specific theological issues to make sure they line up with the beliefs of your church.

3. Listen to God and Adapt

Most importantly, listen to God. Discover what's best for your own particular church and context. You'll want to include in your materials your specific doctrinal slant. God has been uniquely working in your own situation. Adapt the materials according to your own needs.

USING A COMBINATION OF MATERIALS

Many cell churches, while in the process of developing their own materials, use the materials of others. Faith Community Baptist Church uses materials from Ralph Neighbour for their "Year of Equipping." I've noticed, however, that Lawrence Khong and other pastors at FCBC are now writing their own booklets.[8] The Cornerstone Church uses "Year of Equipping" materials, Neil Anderson's materials, Bugbee's Networking materials, and in-house material. For a long time, Bethany World Prayer Center used a series of pamphlets from Christian Equippers alongside their own materials, but now they've developed their own.[9]

CREATE YOUR OWN MATERIALS

Over time, most cell churches establish their own materials because they fit better. God has made your church unique, with particular convictions and methodologies. You'll want to reflect this uniqueness in your material.

14

WHAT WILL YOU
LEAVE BEHIND?

John Wesley and George Whitefield were famous preachers. Each lived during the 18th century and belonged to the same holy club at Oxford University. Both desired to win a lost world for Jesus Christ and were eager to try new methods to do so. In fact, George Whitefield preached in the open air before John Wesley. Most believe that George Whitefield was a better preacher than Wesley. Benjamin Franklin once calculated that Whitefield could easily preach to a crowd of 30,000 people (without a microphone!). Whitefield probably even recorded more decisions than Wesley because of the huge crowds he attracted.

Yet, there were some major differences between the two as well. At the end of his life George Whitefield said this: "My brother Wesley acted wisely — the souls that were awakened under his ministry he joined in class, and thus preserved the fruits of his labor. This I neglected, and my people are a rope of sand."[1]

Historians who wrote about the two men noted that Whitefield's labors died with him while Wesley's fruit continued to grow, increase, and multiply. Wesley left nothing to chance, organizing the movement and bringing it under systematic management; Whitefield hoped that those who had been "awakened" would follow through on their initiative. Wesley raised up a movement that produced leaders, while Whitefield only produced conversions.

Throughout this book, I've encouraged you to act like Wesley, to concentrate on converting your church members into dynamic cell leaders who will produce new cell leaders. Start a movement and you won't have to preside over a monument. View your congregation with leadership eyes and then make sure that you have a training track to prepare them. God wants to use you to spot, train, and release a multitude of leaders.

APPENDIX A

LEADERSHIP ROLES AND FUNCTIONS

The Yoido Full Gospel Church founded and continues to model the Jethro structure. In a nutshell, Cho's Jethro Structure is organized geographically and top leadership use geographical titles: district pastor, zone pastor, section leader, and section supervisor.

This geographical model is used with great effectiveness today. The Elim Church in San Salvador, El Salvador, for example, excels in the "high touch" supervision of top leadership. Each week, zone supervisors, zone pastors, district pastors visit two cell groups per week! Zone pastors meet weekly with supervisors and cell leaders to teach the weekly lesson, so that they in turn can teach it to their groups. Encouragement, motivation, and vision are transmitted during these meetings.

Jethro Structure Minimizes Divisiveness and Doctrinal Error

When I teach cell seminars, I know through experience that someone will ask me about the danger of doctrinal error through cell ministry. "With so many independent meetings in the home, isn't heresy and divisiveness bound to happen?" It's a common fear that cell ministry leads to divisiveness, heresy, and chaos. When asked these questions, I find myself reaffirming the Jethro Structure — that of close supervision in the cell church.

A closely supervised cell church will confront minimal divisiveness. Ralph Neighbour says, "In all the years I pastored a cell group church there was never a single time when a rebellious group set out to become independent and assault the leadership. It rarely happens, and only when communication patterns are poor."[1] Galloway adds, "My testimony is that compared to the healthy, successful groups, the unhealthy ones have been a very small number. Certainly not enough to threaten me so that out of my own insecurity I would stop this mighty work of God in our midst."[2]

Active Involvement of Top Leadership

Cell churches do not rise above the vision of their senior pastors. All eight of my case study churches were led by senior pastors totally committed to cell church philosophy. They navigated their churches through the initial confusion to a clear cell-based philosophy. These pastors believed in delegation, but they refused to delegate the cell church vision. William Beckham says:

Delegation is an important principle in the cell church . . . But — vision and example can't be delegated! Senior church leaders must cast the vision and set the example of living in basic Christian community during the Prototype phase [initiating cell ministry in the church]. The senior leader must model the community he is expecting everyone else to live in. If leaders don't have the time to live together in cell life, how can they expect members to do it?[3]

Senior pastors must be practically involved in cell ministry. Mario Vega, the former senior pastor at the Elim Church, stays actively involved in cell ministry. At the Elim Church, the district pastors, zone pastors, and supervisors weekly visit both a planning meeting on Thursday night and a cell meeting on Saturday night. Why? To remain on the cutting edge of cell ministry. Senior pastors must be the principle supporters of the cell leaders. As Larry Stockstill says, "People will always be interested in what the Senior Pastor is interested in." Stockstill makes sure that he is intimately involved in cell ministry.[4]

At the Republic Church in Quito, Ecuador, all of the directors lead their own cell groups — including Porfirio Ludeña, the senior pastor. I personally lead my own cell group every Thursday night. I don't just want to talk and write about cell ministry, I must experience it. It's one thing to write a book on multiplication. But can I multiply my own cell group?[5] Top leadership must not lose touch with those in the trenches.

THE ELIM CHURCH:
LEADERSHIP ROLES AND FUNCTIONS

The major leadership principle at EC is that all leadership must be in the battle. No one is exempted.[6] EC makes sure that top leadership stays in tune with what is practically happening in cell ministry.

The district pastor, a salaried staff person, is responsible for his entire district. Each district pastor has approximately 675 groups under his care and some 14,500 people. The district pastor principally works with his twelve zone pastors to care for the district. He is regularly involved in preaching (including Sunday morning) and administering the sacraments for his particular district.

The zone pastor, a salaried staff person, oversees the supervisors under his care. He might care for 15 to 30 supervisors. For this reason it is not uncommon for a zone pastor to be responsible for one hundred groups and between 1,000 and 1,500 people. The zone pastor visits his supervisors and cell leaders, preaches during the mid-week service, and administers the sacraments to his zone.[7] The role of supervisor is not a paid position at EC, but it can be a full-time job.[8] Women can be supervisors but only over women's groups.

At EC each leader has only one group. The goal of the cell leader is to multiply that group, which he or she does by developing his or her cell team. The cell leader tries to delegate tasks to every member on the team, so that they in turn will eventually be prepared for cell leadership.

LOVE ALIVE CHURCH: LEADERSHIP ROLES AND FUNCTIONS

The leadership functions are many and varied at LAC. Following are some of the most important responsibilities of the key cell leadership.

The senior pastor oversees the entire cell ministry. He works with the cell director to confirm goals and to plan for the future. He is also available to speak to the cell leaders when called upon. For the most part, however, he is not directly involved with the cell ministry on a weekly basis.

Although the senior pastor is the official head of the cell ministry, the director of the cell ministry is the one who does most of the work. This person pastors the district superintendents, oversees the direction of each district, and coordinates all of the cell ministry activities. As of November 1996, he was the only one on full-time salary.

The district superintendent oversees one of the four geographical districts. As of November 1996, each superintendent had nearly 200 cell groups under his care. He oversees the zone leaders within his district (average of seven zones per district), makes sure that each zone is participating in the activities of the church, and that the goals of the church are being fulfilled. The district superintendent does not visit the cell groups.

When I visited in November 1996, there were 27 zones and zone leaders at LAC. Each zone is broken down into areas, which are cared for by supervisors. The main job of the zone leader, therefore, is to make sure that the area supervisors are growing in the Lord, strengthening the groups under their care, and fulfilling the cell ministry goals.[9]

It appears that the position of the area supervisor is one of the most vital at LAC. This person works individually with the cell leadership teams, and regularly visits the five cell groups under his or her care. The area supervisor must assure that each cell group has a functioning leadership team and that each group is participating in the various activities of the church.

The cell leader is responsible for the care of the cell group. However, in this system he is not alone. The leadership team accompanies him. Therefore, the cell leader must direct both the leadership team and the cell group.

The leadership team is the most fundamental unit at LAC. It is made up of three principle members and two members at large. The team members include the leader, the assistant (preparing to lead the next cell group), the treasurer (counts the money and delivers it to the church each week),[10] and two members at large (who take part in the planning process, serve as replacements, and prepare to fill one of the positions in the new cell group). At LAC, any member of the leadership team is allowed to fulfill any role in the growth group (e.g., lead the lesson, lead worship).

Yoido Full Gospel Church: Leadership Roles and Functions

There are various levels of leadership at YFGC. On the one hand, top leadership meets at the cell level; on the other hand, leadership roles function around the deacon-elder paradigm. Of course, Cho, is the overseer. He writes:

> My job is not going around visiting from house to house and winning individual souls. My job is to oversee the Cell System. I delegate my ministry totally to my associates and to my cell leaders. My job is to mange the training institution, and the training program.[11]

As of March 1995, there were 2,990 senior deacons, 21,169 junior deacons, 3,712 senior deaconesses, 54,596 junior deaconesses, and 919 elders. This can be confusing because there are two leadership branches at YFGC. One works through the cell system (some are paid staff) while the other is volunteer lay leadership that works with, but outside of, the cell system. At first I thought that they were separate entities, but there does seem to be some overlap. District Pastor Yangbae Kim writes:

Each sub-district has 1-5 elders, 15-25 senior deacons and deaconesses, 15-20 Section Leaders and 80-100 Home Cell Leaders. Elders oversee the sub-district and Home Cells, helping the sub-District Pastors. Senior deaconesses are well distributed to the Home Cells.[12]

From this quote it seems that the elders and senior deacons actually oversee districts. Might there be authority conflicts? Pastor Lee assured me that the various leaders submit to one another.

New Hope Community Church: Leadership Roles and Functions

New Hope Community Church promotes three distinct levels of leadership roles. The first level is the trainee. Everyone enters at this level, which lasts about 90 days. The trainee must attend the ongoing weekly training sessions and receives close supervision by the district pastor. The second level is the lay pastor. The lay pastor functions as a cell leader, pastoring the flock under his or her care. The third level is the senior lay pastor. These are the cell leaders who have trained new leadership and multiplied their cell groups. Everyone is encouraged to reach this level.[13]

The International Charismatic Mission: Leadership Functions

ICM breaks the mold of the traditional cell church. This church has decided to follow another drummer. Their entire cell system centers on the concept of the 12.

In this system, there is no need for the elaborate administrative structure found in most cell churches (huge district offices, maps, and mail boxes for each cell leader). Rather, the cell system works effectively at the grass-roots level. It is very simple. Every leader is encouraged to find 12 more leaders. After each of those 12 is active in leading a cell group, he or she spends most of the time caring for that group of 12 (visiting their cell groups, calling them, etc.). The leader of 12 expects that all of his 12 will eventually find their own leaders and also become leaders of 12.

APPLY THE PRINCIPLES

Whatever system you use, make sure that it works for you. Opt for simplicity rather than complexity. The cell roles and functions of the case study churches developed over time. They started with simple structures but required more complexity as their numbers swelled over the 5,000 mark. If you have 100 people in your church and ten cell groups, plan your cell leadership roles accordingly.

Cho's hierarchical model, based on a geographical paradigm, is still the dominant model in the cell church today. That model, however, is giving way to the G-12 paradigm of the ICM church in Bogota, Colombia. Four of my eight case study churches now use this new paradigm (CCG, BWPC, LWC, and ICM).

God doesn't require us to follow molds and methods. Just because it worked in Bogota doesn't necessarily mean it will work in your church. God does ask that we understand the principles behind the methods, so that we might apply them to our own contexts and ministries.

APPENDIX B

LEADERSHIP REQUIREMENTS IN VARIOUS CELL CHURCHES

THE INTERNATIONAL CHARISMATIC MISSION: LEADERSHIP REQUIREMENTS

At ICM, a cell leader must be baptized in water and with the Holy Spirit, and must fulfill the duties of church membership (e.g. attending the main church services, tithing, and demonstrating faithfulness to the church).[1]

LEADERSHIP REQUIREMENTS AT ICM

1. Baptized in water and with the Holy Spirit
2. Fulfill the duties of church membership (e.g. attending the main church services, tithing, and demonstrating faithfulness to the church)
3. Encounter Retreat
4. Three month training course for leadership
5. Second Encounter Retreat

Holy living is repeatedly emphasized along with maintaining a godly family life. The top leadership does not hesitate to remove people who are not living godly lives. I repeatedly heard stories of leaders being removed because they were living in sin or were in ministry because of their talent instead of their commitment to Christ. I heard of several leaders being removed or strongly warned about having a "spirit of pride." They were not submissive to those in charge.

Youth leaders multiply their cell group in order to remain in leadership. One example of this is the drummer who was given one month to multiply his cell group or resign. Supposedly, he was in leadership because of his talent and not a heart for ministry. He resigned. I'm reminded that John Wesley did not hesitate to remove "class" leaders if they were not living in holiness.

CHRISTIAN CENTER OF GUAYAQUIL: LEADERSHIP REQUIREMENTS

Leadership requirements at CCG include salvation, baptism in water, attendance at a cell group, and completion of the four-week cell leader-training course. Although an Assembly of God church, it did not require that the cell leader speak in tongues. According to a manual distributed at the 1997 CCG conference, the requirements for a cell leader at CCG are:[2]

LEADERSHIP REQUIREMENTS AT CCG

1. Baptism in water
2. Membership (Faithfulness in time and offering at CCG)
3. Form part of the leadership team of the cell group
4. Attend the leadership course for cell leaders
5. Godly Christian living
6. Maintain a godly family life

BETHANY WORLD PRAYER CENTER: LEADERSHIP REQUIREMENTS

All cell leaders must fulfill the following requirements before entering leadership at BWPC:[3]

LEADERSHIP REQUIREMENTS AT BWPC

1. Be saved and exemplify a strong Christian life	6. Complete all discipleship and leadership requirements
2. Be a faithful member of Bethany World Prayer Center for six months, having submitted to the leadership at Bethany	7. If married, your spouse must be in agreement with your working in the Touch Group Ministry
	8. Be recommended by the cell leader for cell leader
3. Be a member of a BWPC Touch Group	9. Be interviewed by District/Zone Pastor
4. Be baptized in the Holy Spirit	a. DISC evaluation
5. Be a faithful tither of your income to the Lord	b. Enjoy Sheet/spiritual gifts
	c. Analysis of their leadership file

The District Pastor accepts the application for leadership. Beyond these basic requirements lies the cell leaders' training, which has been discussed previously.

ELIM CHURCH: LEADERSHIP REQUIREMENTS

The leadership requirements are minimal at EC. They include six months of being a Christian, membership in a cell group, baptism in the Holy Spirit, baptism in water, and completion of the four-week leadership training.

LEADERSHIP REQUIREMENTS AT EC

1. Six months of being a Christian
2. Membership in a cell group
3. Baptism in the Holy Spirit
4. Baptism in water
5. Completion of the four-week leadership training.

The heaviest requirement after entering cell leadership is the time commitment. I calculated that the cell leader (as well as the supervisor) must attend five meetings per week.[4] On top of that there are additional commitments such as visitation, all-night prayer meetings, fasting days, and weekly statistical reporting.[5]

FAITH COMMUNITY BAPTIST CHURCH: LEADERSHIP REQUIREMENTS

Pre-Leadership Requirements
All potential leaders must pass a number of hurdles before entering cell leadership. The process is called the "year of equipping," but I can imagine that it might take longer than one year. Another name for training at FCBC is Touch Equipping Stations System (TESS). The 1997 TESS brochure states:

> The term 'Equipping Stations' underscores an important aspect of the training philosophy of FCBC. The equipping process adopted by FCBC is likened to a subway system where commuters get on and off stations along a particular line in order to get to an intended destination. No one stays in a particular station for long. Likewise TESS has a very clear end

in mind — equipping FCBC's members for ministry. A member goes to a particular station for a very specific purpose and leaves it once he has been equipped for that purpose. He does not go to another equipping station until he needs to be further equipped for ministry.

Recommendation by Cell Leader

This is the first requirement. The cell leader must recommend the potential cell leader. Cell leaders are looking for FAST people (faithful, available, submissive, and teachable).

Cell Leader Intern Training

This course lasts for nine weeks and is usually taught by a zone pastor. The course covers the cell church, the cell agenda, worship time in the cell, word time and works time in the cell, cell life, prayer, and leadership. A potential cell leader must complete this course before officially becoming a cell leader.

Internship for Six Months

After the intern completes the basic nine-week training, he or she must serve as the cell leader intern for six months before becoming the official cell leader. When the group multiplies, the intern is then ready to take the new group. In the past (1993), they have asked each leader to stay on the job until the cell multiplied two times, but I didn't hear this requirement mentioned when I was present.

LEADERSHIP REQUIREMENTS AT FCBC

1. Pre-Leadership Requirements ("year of equipping")
2. Recommendation by Cell Leader
3. Cell Leader Intern Training (nine weeks)
4. Internship for six months

LOVE ALIVE CHURCH: LEADERSHIP REQUIREMENTS

If one decides to be involved in cell ministry, he or she must be a Christian for two years, be a regular member of a cell group for one year, be the assistant cell leader first, be baptized in water and in the Spirit, pass an interview with the district supervisor, enroll in the discipleship training, and have the proper disposition (e.g., correct attitudes, good testimony, submission to authority).

Nothing is done hurriedly or whimsically at LAC. It is possible that this is the reason that their cell groups have experienced consistent growth. Unlike other cell ministries in which leaders often have two or more groups, at LAC each leader may direct only one group.[6]

LEADERSHIP REQUIREMENTS AT LAC

1. Christian for two years
2. Regular member of a cell group for one year
3. Service as assistant cell leader
4. Baptism in water and in the Spirit
5. Pass the interview with the district supervisor
6. Enrollment in the discipleship training
7. Proper disposition (e.g., correct attitudes, good testimony, submission to authority).

YOIDO FULL GOSPEL CHURCH: LEADERSHIP REQUIREMENTS

There are various qualifications to become a cell leader. District Pastor Yangbae Kim writes, "The qualifications to become a Home Cell Leader are regular attendance at church services, giving tithes, fullness of the Holy Spirit, and devotional posture." In an in-depth interview with District Pastor Song Ho Lee, I learned that a potential leader must first attend the church for more than three years, be baptized in water and in the Spirit (with the evidence of speaking in tongues), and attend the worship services faithfully.[7]

Interestingly enough, he told me that there are no educational requirements specifically for cell leaders. I learned that the educational training at YFGC is for everyone. Pastor Lee told me that it is preferred that all potential cell leaders receive Christian education at YFGC, but it was not mandatory in order to become a leader.

LEADERSHIP REQUIREMENTS AT YFGC

1. Regular attendance at church services
2. Faithful tither
3. Fullness of the Holy Spirit
4. Devotional posture
5. Attendance at the church for at least three years
6. Baptism in water and in the Spirit (with the evidence of speaking in tongues)

New Hope Community Church: Leadership Requirements

All leaders at NHCC sign a one-year renewable contract to serve both as group leader and lay pastor. The time requirement for a typical leader at NHCC is six to eight hours per week. Hunter writes:

> Lay pastors and assistant lay pastors must first take a weekend of training before assuming leadership of any group. Once involved as leaders, they are expected to attend a weekly leaders' meeting — where they submit reports from last week's meeting, study the lesson for their next group meeting, and receive further training in lay ministry and small group leadership."[8]

New Hope expects their leaders to file weekly reports as well as attend weekly training meetings.[9] Here are the 12 requirements that NHCC asks of their leaders:[10]

LEADERSHIP REQUIREMENTS AT NHCC

1. Consistency and commitment to leading the Christian lifestyle
2. Vision and loyalty to the church
3. Dependability and accountability to leadership
4. Consistent walk with the Holy Spirit
5. Regular participant or leader of a small group
6. Commitment to attend the lay-pastor's weekly training meeting (they have six or seven different weekly training schedules each week)
7. Commitment to wear the lay-pastor's badge on Sunday
8. Discipleship of those who come forward during the celebration services
9. Faithful and diligent work each week
10. Membership in the church
11. Faithfulness in tithing to the church
12. Maintain a solid family life

NOTES

Introduction

[1] Gwynn Lewis, "Time Bombs that Kill a Cell," *CellChurch Magazine*, Summer 1995, 10.

[2] *Cell Leader Intern Guidebook* (Houston: TOUCH Publications, Inc., 1995), 101.

[3] Jim Egli, "The Ten Commandments of Transitions," *CellChurch Magazine*, Summer 1996, 14.

[4] Most books on Christian leadership agree that leadership is influence. Dr. Bobby Clinton defines leadership like this: "A leader, as defined from a study of Biblical leadership, . . . is a person, with God-given capacity and with God-given responsibility who is influencing a specific group of God's people toward God's purposes for the group" *(Leadership Perspectives* (Altadena, CA: Barnabas Publishers, 1993), 14). Wagner uses the idea of influencing a group of people towards God's purpose to define the "gift of leadership" in the New Testament (Rom. 12:8). He says: The gift of leadership is the special ability that God gives to certain members of the Body of Christ to set goals in accordance with God's purpose for the future and to communicate these goals to others in such a way that they voluntarily and harmoniously work together to accomplish those goals for the glory of God"(*Your Spiritual Gifts Can Help Your Church Grow* (Ventura, CA: Regal Books, 1979), 162). The TOUCH Outreach seminar for zone supervisors describes a leader as, ". . . a person who **encourages** others, who **motivates** others to meet the group goals . . ."(*Zone Supervisor Seminar* (Houston: TOUCH Outreach Ministries, 1997), F-1). In this book, I will follow the above consensus that a leader is one who influences a particular group to meet its goal.

[5] Robert J. Clinton, *Leadership Perspectives* (Altadena, CA: Barnabas Publishers, 1993), 14.

Chapter 1
[1] Barna Research Group (Ventura, Calif.) *Morrock News Digest*, <http://morrock.com>12/8/1999.
[2] James Lardner, "World-class Workaholics," *U.S. News & World Report*, <http://www.usnews.com/usnews/issue/991220/overwork.htm>, (12/20/1999).
[3] "Study: Americans Work Longest Hours," *Infobeat Morning Coffee Edition* (9/7/1999), <http://www.infobeat.com> (9/7/1999). The report was based on figures covering the years 1980-1997. On average, U.S. workers clocked up 1,966 hours at work in the most recent year, the study said. In 1980, the average was 1,883 hours.
[4] Geert Hofstede, *Culture's Consequence* (Beverly Hills, CA: Sage Publications, 1980), 230-231.
[5] Paul D. Stanley & J. Robert Clinton, *Connecting: The Mentoring Relationships You Need to Succeed in Life* (Colorado Springs, CO: NavPress, 1992), 12.
[6] Carl George, *Prepare Your Church for the Future* (Grand Rapids, MI: Fleming H. Revell, 1992), 98.

Chapter 2
[1] John Maxwell, *Developing the Leader within You* (Nashville: Thomas Nelson Publishers, 1993), 80.
[2] Peter Wagner, *Your Church Can Grow* (Ventura, CA: Regal Books, 1976), 91.
[3] David Yonggi Cho, *Successful Home Cell Groups* (Plainfield, NJ: Logos International, 1981), 21-32.
[4] Larry Stockstill, "Leadership Base Path," message given at 1998 National Cell Church Pastor's Conference in Baker, Louisiana, audio tape.
[5] I visited YFGC in April, 1997, and these were the current statistics. The District Pastor is always male but the vast majority of Zone Pastors (sub-District Pastors) are female. This fact became obvious to me as I walked from district office to district office.
[6] Dale Galloway, *20/20 Vision* (Portland, OR: Scott Publishing Company, 1986), 132.
[7] William Brown, "Growing the Church Through Small Groups in the Australian Context," D.Min. dissertation (Pasadena, CA: Fuller Theological Seminary, 1992), 39.
[8] Howard A. Snyder, *The Radical Wesley* (Downers Grove, IL: Inter-Varsity Press, 1980), 57,63 as quoted in Larry Kreider, *House to House* (Houston: TOUCH Publications, 1995), 24.
[9] For complete information on this topic, please read my book, *Home Cell Group Explosion: How Your Small Group Can Grow and Multiply* (Houston: TOUCH Publications, 1998). In a nutshell, I discovered that successful cell leaders, who multiplied their group, spent more time seeking God's face, depending on Him for the direction of their cell group. They prepared themselves first and only afterwards, the lesson. They prayed diligently for their members, as well as non-Christian contacts. But successful cell leaders did not stop with prayer. They came down from the mountaintop to interact with real people, full of problems and pain. They pastored their cell members, visiting them regularly. They refused to allow the obstacles — that all cell leaders face — to overcome them. They fastened their eyes on one goal — reaching a lost world for Jesus through cell multiplication.
[10] Used with permission from "Quest for the Perfect Pastoral System," 4. Pastor Harold F. Weitsz is the pastor of Little Fall Christian Centre, Little Falls, Roodepoort, South Africa. Presently, there are 2500 members and 200 cells.

Chapter 3
[1] César Castellanos, *Transitioning to the Cell Church Philosophy*, audiotape.
[2] Carl George, *The Coming Church Revolution* (Grand Rapids, MI: Fleming H. Revell, 1994), 48.

Chapter 4
[1] John Maxwell, *Developing the Leader within You.* 146.

[2] Herb Miller, *The Empowered Leader: 10 Keys to Servant Leadership* (Nashville, Tennessee: Broadman & Holman Publishers,1995), 27.

[3] I wrote down leadership characteristics from five books and noted their differences:

Spiritual Leadership by J. Oswald Sanders	Leadership that Endures In a World That Changes by John Haggai	Leadership Style of Jesus by Michael Youssef	Learn to Be a Leader by G.S. Dobbins	Leaders are Made: Not Born by Ted Engstrom
• Discipline • Vision • Wisdom • Decisiveness • Courage • Humility • Integrity • Humor • Patience • Friendship • Prudence • Inspirational • Decision maker • Listener • Prayer Warrior • Reader • Organizer	• Vision • Goal Setter • Lover • Humility • Self Control • Risk Taker • High Energy • Perseverance • Authority • Knowledge	• Courage • Friendliness • Tradition breaker • Generous • Truthful • Forgiving	• Good health • Physically attractive • Intelligent • Superior education • Clear ideals • Enthusiastic • Perseverance • Capacity to learn • Integrity • Good reputation • Faithful	• Integrity • Visionary • Willingness to deal with obstacles • Ability to receive correction • Flexible • Committed to people

[4] Warren Bennis & Burt Nanus, *Leaders: The Strategies for Taking Charge* (New York: Harper Perennial, 1985), 20.

[5] Ibid., 4.

[6] *Zone Supervisor Seminar* (Houston: TOUCH Outreach Ministries, 1997), F-1.

[7] Gareth Weldon Icenogle, *Biblical Foundations for Small Group Ministry* (Downer's Grove, IL: InterVarsity Press, 1994), 179.

[8] Herb Miller, *The Empowered Leader: 10 Keys to Servant Leadership.*

[9] Quoted in *CellChurch Magazine*, Summer 1996, 8.

[10] Steve Barker, Judy Johnson, Rob Malone, Ron Nicholas, & Doug Whallon, *Good Things Come in Small Groups* (Downers Grove, IL, 1985), 44.

[11] TABLE: AVERAGE REQUIREMENT FOR CHRISTIAN COMMITMENT

THREE MONTHS—CCG	ONE YEAR—FCBC
THREE MONTHS—ICM	ONE YEAR—LWC
SIX MONTHS—BWPC	TWO YEARS—LAC
SIX MONTHS-EC	THREE YEARS—YFGC

[12] *The American Heritage Dictionary of the English Language,* 3rd ed., s.v. "value."

[13] *The Original Roget's Thesaurus of English Words and Phrases,* s.v. "value."

Chapter 5

[1] James M. Kourzes & Barry Z. Posner, *The Leadership Challenge: How to Keep Getting Extraordinary Things Done in Organizations* (San Francisco, CA: Jossey-Bass Publishers, 1995), 9-10.

[2] Stephen Pile, *The Book of Failures*, quoted in Terry Powell, *You Can Lead a Bible Discussion Group!* (Sisters, OR: Mulnomah Books, 1996), 14.

[3] Taken from the article by Greg Lee, "The Key to Growth: Multiplication," *CellChurch Magazine*, Winter 1996, 15.

[4] James M. Kouzes & Barry Z. Posner, 69.

[5] Michael Lewis, "The Cult of Failure in the Silicon Valley," *Slate Magazine*. Internet, Jan. 21, 1998.

[6] John Maxwell, *The 21 Irrefutable Laws of Leadership* (Nashville, TN: Thomas Nelson Publishing, 1998), 27.

[7] Fraternidad Cristiana de Guatemala, *El Perfil de un Líder* (Guatemala), 1.

[8] John Maxwell, *Developing the Leader within You*, 164.

[9] Ibid., 165.

[10] Bill Gates, *Business @ the Speed of Thought: Using a Digital Nervous System* (New York: Warner Books, 1999), 470.

[11] Donald McGavran, *Understanding Church Growth* 3rd ed. (Grand Rapids, MI: William B. Eerdmans Publishing Co., 1990), 265.

[12] I've personally heard Wagner make this comment at Fuller Theological Seminary. The context for the statement was church growth — pastors who produce little but work day and night. Wagner taught the importance of focused, strategic work.

[13] David Yonggi Cho, *Church Growth Manual* No. 7 (Seoul, Korea: Church Growth International, 1995), 18.

[14] Ibid.

[15] "Ministerio de Profesionales," *Manual Operativo Células*, International Charismatic Mission, 1996.

[16] Much of the church growth success that we experienced at the El Batán Church in Quito, Ecuador had to do with the passion that possessed the leadership team to set clear, specific church growth goals and then to visibly display those goals on a huge plastic poster board.

[17] William A. Beckham, *The Second Reformation* (Houston: TOUCH Publications, 1995), 223.

[18] Stephen R. Covey, *The 7 Habits of Highly Effective People* (New York: Simon and Schuster, 1989), 101-106.

[19] As quoted in Michael E. Gerber, *The E Myth* (New York: HarperBusiness, 1995), 69.

[20] Rick Warren, *How To Build A Purpose Driven Church* (Saddleback Seminar Workbook, 1995), 10.

[21] On the other hand, Barna in his book, *The Power of Vision* (Ventura, CA: Regal Books, 1992), advises the leader not to use slogans. He feels that slogans have a tendency to trivialize the vision rather than simplify it (140). One of the subheadings reads, "Shelve the Slogans" (139).

[22] George Barna, *The Power of Vision* (Ventura, CA: Regal Books, 1992), 143.

[23] As we transitioned at the Republic Church from a church with cells to a cell church in 1997-1998, some leaders "felt" that we were making too many announcements about our cell church identity. The constant barrage of announcements, however, solidified our new cell church identity and gave people a clear understanding of our new direction. Within seven months, we tripled the number of cell groups and doubled cell attendance.

[24] This seems to be a constant problem among Latin leadership. When working through their goals for the future, I have noticed a tendency to be highly unrealistic.

[25] Burt Nanus, *Visionary Leadership* (San Francisco, CA: Jossey Boss Publications, 1992), 159-161.

[26] David Yonggi Cho, *Church Growth Manual* No. 7, 27.

Chapter 6

[1] John Maxwell, *Developing the Leaders Around You*, 3.

[2] David J. Bosch, "The Structure of Mission: An Exposition of Matthew 28:16-20" *Exploring Church Growth* ed. Wilbert R. Shenk (Grand Rapids, MI: Eerdmans, 1983), 228-233.

[3] Robert Wuthnow, *Sharing the Journey* (New York: The Free Press, 1994), 246.

[4] George Hunter III, *Church for the Unchurched* (Nashville: Abingdon Press, 1996), 101.

5 Ibid., 97.

6 David Yonggi Cho, *Church Growth Manual* No. 7, 19.

7 Karen Hurston, *Growing the World's Largest Church* (Springfield, MI: Chrism, 1995), 102-105.

8 Ibid., 218. This was a survey taken in 1987. All of us can learn from the example of YFGC. Apart from fervent prayer, their amazing cell group success has resulted from consistent, planned visitation. As I visited the cell offices at YFGC and spent time talking to the district leaders, I noticed a clear pattern — District Pastors and sub-District Pastors spend the majority of their time in visitation. In fact, the only required weekly report at YFGC records the number and type of visits that each District Pastor performed. Cell leadership around the world would do well to learn from their example. Discipleship of new believers is intimately related to cell visitation at YFGC. The sub-District Pastor and the Section Leader visit the new convert. They share testimonies with the new believer and invite him to receive Christ in their presence. These new converts are placed in the most appropriate cell based on age, civil status, and location. The Christian Center of Guayaquil has followed Cho's example of diligent, consistent visitation. Zone leaders at CCG make about 40 visits each week. This amounts to approximately 920 visits by all of the zone leaders each week. These visits are directed to the cell members, new converts, and visitors to the church, in that order. The Zone Pastor is always alert to the possibility of opening a new home for a cell group, a future leader, or the possibility of forming two cell groups. Many of the new groups start as a result of the diligent visits by Zone Pastors.

9 The International Charismatic Mission has a complete manual dedicated to instructing cell leaders how to visit systematically.

Chapter 7
1 Jim Egli and Paul M. Zehr, *Alternative Models of Mennonite Pastoral Formation* (Elkhart, IN: Institute of Mennonite Studies, 1992), 43.

2 Ibid., 41.

Chapter 8
1 Howard Hendricks, *As Iron Sharpens Iron* (Chicago: Moody Press, 1995), 26.

2 Shirley Peddy, *The Art of Mentoring: Lead, Follow, and Get Out of the Way* (Houston: Bullion Books, 1998), 24.

3 Robert Clinton, *The Mentor Handbook* (Pasadena, CA: Barnabas Publishers, 1991), ch.2, 3.

4 Ibid.

5 Adapted from Paul D. Stanley & J. Robert Clinton, *Connecting: The Mentoring Relationships You Need to Succeed in Life* (Colorado Springs, CO: NavPress, 1992), 42.

6 Ibid., 94.

7 Howard Hendricks, 28.

8 Ibid., 27.

9 Shirley Peddy, 46.

10 Robert Clinton, *The Mentor Handbook,* ch. 2, 17.

11 James Flaherty, *Coaching: Evoking Excellence in Others* (Boston, Butterworth-Heinemann, 1999), 11.

12 Mark Jobe, "Chicago Style Disciple-Making," *CellChurch Magazine*, Summer 1995, 6.

Chapter 9
1 Bill Gates, 380.

2 P. Hersey and K. Blanchard, *Management of Organizational Behavior* (New Jersey, Prentice Hall, 1988), 170.

3 Icenogle, 166-167.

[4] Ibid., 167.

[5] P. Hersey and K. Blanchard, 182.

[6] C. Peter Wagner, *Leading Your Church to Growth* (Ventura, CA: Regal Books,1984), 59.

[7] Ibid., 58.

[8] Carl George, *Prepare Your Church for the Future*, 67.

[9] C. Peter Wagner, *Leading Your Church to Growth*, 58-59.

[10] Carl George, *How To Break Growth Barriers* (Grand Rapids, MI: Baker Book House, 1993), 85-108.

[11] Ibid., 105.

[12] In many cell churches today, there are upper levels of management, so that the pastor actually trains for those who are over five cells, etc. and not the actual cell leaders personally.

[13] J. Robert Clinton, *The Making of a Leader* (Colorado Springs, CO: NavPress, 1988), 23. The leaders that Clinton and his students have studied include biblical characters, historical Christian leaders, and contemporary leaders.

[14] Ibid., 33.

[15] Ibid., 115.

[16] Ibid., 83.

Chapter 10

[1] Neal F. McBride, *How to Build a Small Groups Ministry* (Colorado Springs, CO: NavPress, 1995), 128.

[2] Ralph W. Neighbour Jr., "7 Barriers to Growth," *CellChurch Magazine*, Summer 1997, 16.

[3] Carl George, *The Coming Church Revolution*, 79.

[4] Carl George, *Prepare Your Church for the Future*, 135.

[5] Paul Benjamin quoted in Michael Mack, *The Synergy Church* (Grand Rapids, MI: Baker Books, 1996), 64.

[6] George Hunter III, 120-121.

[7] Randall Neighbour, "Virus Eats Leaders, Kills Cells," *CellChurch Magazine*, Summer 1997, 8.

[8] Bill Donahue, *Leading Life-Changing Small Groups* (Grand Rapids, MI: Zondervan, 1996), 75.

[9] Carl George, *The Coming Church Revolution*, 46.

[10] Glen Martin & Gary McIntosh, *Creating Community* (Nashville: Broadman & Holman Publishers, 1997), 113.

[11] Randall Neighbour, 8.

[12] Barbara J. Fleischer, *Facilitating for Growth* (Collegeville, MN: The Liturgical Press, 1993), 21.

[13] Ralph W. Neighbour Jr., *The Shepherd's Guidebook* (Houston: TOUCH Publications, 1992), 131.

[14] Most of these techniques were taken from Neal F. McBride, *How to Build a Small Groups Ministry* (Colorado Springs, CO: NavPress, 1995), 127. I mixed the order and added the #4-retreat.

[15] Ralph W. Neighbour Jr., *Where Do We Go From Here?* (Houston: TOUCH Publications, 1990), 361-362.

[16] Ralph W. Neighbour Jr., personal e-mail, (1/18/1998). About the classroom training at FCBC he wrote, ". . . at the stage of becoming a Cell Leader, we have a parallel to Cesar's classes [the ICM model] to train them. Eight weeks of two hour sessions are developed, and I have written 3 books for the cell leader plus a leader's guide."

[17] My own mentor, Peter Wagner, only teaches week-long intensives at Fuller Theological Seminary. His busy schedule doesn't permit him to teach weekly over a period of three to four weeks.

[18] When my wife and I began the cell system in Ecuador, I followed a small manual that we received from a fellow missionary who was the senior pastor of a C&MA church in Colombia. The manual recommended holding ongoing bimonthly training sessions with all cell leadership. We followed the general tenor of that model throughout our time in Ecuador. Before leaving

Ecuador, a key co-worker (a fellow missionary with whom I had worked side-by-side in the cell ministry) and I reflected back on 3 years of cell ministry. Both of us agreed that the ongoing training sessions were the backbone of our cell ministry. In my own cell manual, I call this bimonthly meeting, "the motor" of the cell group ministry.

[19] Floyd L. Schwanz, *Growing Small Groups* (Kansas City, MO: Beacon Hill Press, 1995), 122.

[20] Ibid., 121. Schwanz divides this time into inspiration, information, and illustration (modeling the cell). Speaking of the information time, Schwanz says, "Coming together once each week actually is a time-saver for the leaders. Their preparation time is almost nothing. After training, they can go right out and lead a group without doing any homework."

[21] Paul Yonggi Cho, *Successful Home Cell Groups,* 136.

[22] Neal F. McBride, *How to Build a Small Groups Ministry,* 174.

[23] This training might be weekly, bimonthly, or monthly. Actually, I have found that every three weeks is probably the best option.

Chapter 11

[1] The *Track Pack* from TOUCH Publications consist of a series of books (pamphlets).

[2] Ralph W. Neighbour Jr., *The Arrival Kit* (Houston: TOUCH Publications, 1993), 11.

[3] In the *Track Pack* (TOUCH Publications) you find the book for all levels of training.

[4] Ralph W. Neighbour Jr., *Welcome To Your Changed Life* (Houston: TOUCH Publications, 1995) 14.

[5] Ralph W. Neighbour Jr., *The Arrival Kit,* 41.

[6] Ibid., 41.

[7] Ralph W. Neighbour Jr., *The Shepherd's Guidebook,* 26.

[8] Ralph W. Neighbour Jr., *The Sponsor's Guidebook* (Houston: TOUCH Publications, 1995), 5.

[9] Ibid., 22-32.

[10] All of these booklets are available from TOUCH Outreach Ministries, Inc./P.O. Box 19888/ Houston, TX, 77224/ 281-497-7901. TOUCH's web site is simply: http://www.touchusa.org. Their toll free number for ordering books is 1-800-735-5865.

[11] *Oikos* is the Greek word for house or household in the New Testament. Four booklets of the Track Pack focus on teaching the new believer to reach out to non-Christians.

[12] Ralph W. Neighbour Jr., *The Shepherd's Guidebook,* 27.

[13] Ralph W. Neighbour Jr., *Where Do We Go From Here?,* 251.

[14] Ralph W. Neighbour Jr., *Building Groups Opening Hearts* (Houston: TOUCH Publications, 1991), 60.

[15] Ralph W. Neighbour Jr., *The Shepherd's Guidebook,* 73.

[16] Ralph W. Neighbour Jr., *Welcome To Your Changed Life,* 4

[17] Ralph W. Neighbour Jr., *Where Do We Go From Here?,* 367.

[18] Written by a team of pastors, *Discipleship 201* (Baker, LA: Bethany World Prayer Center, 1998), 4.

[19] Larry Stockstill, "Leadership Base Path," message given at 1998 National Cell Church Pastor's Conference in Baker, Louisiana, audio tape.

[20] César Castellanos, *Sueña y Ganarás el Mundo* (Bogota, Colombia: Vilit Editorial, 1998), 104 and José Maria Villanueva, *El Desarrollo de los Encuentros,* Audio tape.

[21] Claudia Castellanos, *Encuentro: La Base del Discipulado,* Audio tape.

[22] Mercedes de Acevedo, *Formando para Formar,* Audio tape.

[23] In October 1996, attendance at a second Encounter Retreat was only a requirement for the youth cells group leaders. By March 1997 the whole church required the second retreat. It is common knowledge at ICM that the ministry of the young people is the most effective in the entire church. I heard from several leaders that ideas and methods are first proven among the young people and if they work they are implemented in the entire church.

[24] Latin Americans, along with most face-to-face/family oriented cultures, are very group oriented. They think and act as a group, as opposed to individuals. North Americans, on the other hand, are very individualistic. The best research on this is, Geert Hofstede, *Culture's Consequence* (Beverly Hills, CA: Sage Publications, 1980). Hofstede's research of 30+ cultures proved that North Americans are the most individualistic society on earth, whereas Latinos tend to be among most group oriented.

[25] This information comes from a communiqué entitled "Praying and Dreaming Summit of Cell Church Networks in Hong Kong," held in mid-November, 1997. (Neville Chamberlain, "Cell Church Missions Network Roundup #14." November 21, 1997. E-mail received from Ralph W. Neighbour on November 22, 1997). The communiqué said that in just 3 months, since putting the new plan into action, the church experienced an amazing mini-revival. About 130 people came to the Lord, 70 were baptized, and 28 new cell groups formed. My attempts to contact Pastor Raj to obtain current statistics have failed.

[26] Floyd L. Schwanz, 120.

[27] Those churches in the U.S. using the Meta Model often substitute the weekly Huddle for a bimonthly or even monthly Huddle. The Huddle continues to be a very important affair.

[28] Those following the Meta Model of small group ministry normally demonstrate a commitment to these small group values: Variety of groups (little similarity among groups — task group, special interest groups, closed groups, open groups, recovery groups, etc.), Flexibility (with regard to material, group multiplication, length of group life, etc.), Jethro Model (administrative system is structured around Exodus 18), Small groups mix with support additional church programs.

[29] I have classified Saddleback Church under the Meta Model due to the characteristics of Saddleback's small group ministry. However, the church does not officially line up with any particular model.

[30] Carl George, *The Coming Church Revolution*, 83.

[31] At this time, very few Meta Churches insist on bimonthly ongoing leadership training (since the Meta Model has now been proven in the market place).

[32] Carl George, *Prepare Your Church for the Future*, 121-148.

[33] George G. Hunter III, 95.

[34] Ibid., 92.

[35] There are no outside Bible classes, TEE, or Bible institute training. Membership is taught from a certain interpretation of Scripture without much further exposure. Although each cell leader preaches with loud fervor, there is not a lot of "in-depth" Biblical preparation.

Chapter 12

[1] Paul Lee Tan, "Epigram" *Encyclopedia of 7700 Illustrations* (Rockville, Maryland: Assurance Publishers, 1980), 722.

Chapter 13

[1] TOUCH materials can be purchased from TOUCH Outreach Ministries, Inc./P.O. Box 19888/ Houston, TX, 77224/ 281-497-790. TOUCH's web site is simply: http://www.touchusa.org. Their phone number to order books is 1-800-735-5865.

[2] J. Peters Thomas, *Thriving on Chaos* (New York: Harper Perennial,1987), 284.

[3] Ibid.

[4] Contact the International Charismatic Mission by telephone at (571) 565-7708, 337-9211; Fax (571) 269-6172; E-mail: mci@latino.net.co.

[5] Contact Little Falls Christian Centre at lfcc@iafrica.com . Their web site is: http://www.cellchurchint.co.za/ or http://www.lfcc.co.za/.

6 The phone number of BWPC is 504-774-1700. For material/tapes, ask for Montie Pitts (MPitts@bethany.com).

7 Volume 1 is entitled *The Home Cell Group Study Guide* (Milton Keynes, England: Word Publishing, 1990) by David Yonggi Cho. There are now several volumes available.

8 One example is a book edited by Lawrence Khong called *Type A Evangelism Training Workbook* (Singapore: TOUCH Resource P/L, 1996). TOUCH Ministries International of Singapore now distributes its own cell material to many parts of Asia and around the world. They can be reached by phone at 65-346-9020, Fax-65-345-6415 or e-mail: tmirong@singnet.com.sg.

9 Christian Equippers International can be reached at 1-800-662-0909 or 916-542-1509, or by e-mail: Equip@Oakweb.com.

Chapter 14

1 D. Michael Henderson, *John Wesley's Class Meetings: A Model for Making Disciples* (Nappanee, IN: Evangel Publishing House, 1997), 30.

Appendix A

1 Ralph W. Neighbour Jr., *Where Do We Go From Here?*, 73.

2 Dale E. Galloway, *20/20 Vision*, 156.

3 William A. Beckham, *The Second Reformation*, 168.

4 He visits a cell each week; he writes the cell material, he gives the vision to the leaders in the monthly summit, etc.

5 Thus far, I've multiplied my own cell group four times and my goal for 2000 is to multiply it two more times.

6 I was very impressed by the commitment of Jorge Galindo to the cell ministry (the previous senior pastor). He realized that the head pastor is the key to the success of the cell ministry, and he was involved in weekly planning meetings with the District Pastors, weekly encouragement of the Zone Pastors, and weekly attendance in a cell.

7 Unlike some cell churches, the Zone Pastors at EC are not encouraged to visit a set number of people.

8 The supervisor has five required meetings that he or she must attend each week.

9 More recently at LAC it was determined that the zone leader needs to have more contact with the cell groups. It appears that this role had become more administrative. The zone leaders were not supposed to visit the cell groups, and thus it seems that their effectiveness was diminished. LAC is trying to correct this problem.

10 At times the administration might have a meeting of all the treasurers to share a pressing financial need in the church. All of the money received in the group goes directly to the church, with the exception of those groups who need to contract buses for the Saturday service. In that case, every other offering is for the church. Treasurers are entrusted to receive the tithes and offerings of the people.

11 David Yonggi Cho, *Church Growth. Manual* No.7, 21.

12 Peggy L. Kannaday, P.L., ed., *Church Growth and the Home Cell System* (Seoul, Korea: Church Growth International, 1995), 128.

13 Dale Galloway, *20/20 Vision*, 133-134.

Appendix B

1 The baptism of the Holy Spirit is evidenced by speaking in tongues at ICM.

2 *Curso de Formación de Líderes en una Iglesia de Células*, Centro Cristiano de Guayaquil, Ecuador, August, 1997, 14.

[3] Application copy of qualifications for leadership *Bethany Cell Conference manual*, June, 1996.

[4] Monday, expository teaching service; Tuesday, Zone Pastor meeting with supervisors and cell leaders; Thursday, cell planning meeting; Saturday, cell meeting, and Sunday, normal services.

[5] Time-wise, it seems much easier to be a zone or District Pastor than a cell leader or supervisor.

[6] This same principle applies to the cell members, who are allowed to attend only one cell group.

[7] From Hurston's observations, only Section Leaders are required to speak in tongues (1995:76). She also notes that to become a Section Leader, in contrast with a cell leader, one must be a cell leader for at least two years (1995:75).

[8] George G. Hunter III, 88.

[9] Ibid., 92.

[10] Dale Galloway, *The Small Group Book* (Grand Rapids, MI: Fleming H. Revell, 1995), 90-92.

INDEX

ADDITIONAL RESOURCES
by Joel Comiskey

GROUPS OF 12
This book clears the confusion about the Groups of 12 model. Joel has dug deeply into the International Charismatic Mission in Bogota Columbia and other G-12 churches to learn the simply principles that G-12 has to offer your church. This book also contrasts the G-12 model with the classic 5x5 structure and shows you what to do with this new model of ministry. 182 pgs.

FROM 12 TO 3
There are two basic ways to embrace the G-12 concept: adopting the entire model or applying the principles that support the model. This book focuses on the second. It provides you with a modified approach called the "G-12.3." This approach presents a workable pattern that is adaptable to many different church and cultural contexts, including your unique environment. 184 pgs.

REAP THE HARVEST
This book casts a vision for cell groups that will work in your church. Based on research of the best cell churches around the world and practical experience by the author, Reap the Harvest will reveal the 16 proven principles behind cell-church growth and effectiveness. It will also provide you with a strong biblical and historical foundation that anyone can understand. Great to share with key leaders as you transition to cell groups. 240 pgs.

HOME CELL GROUP EXPLOSION
This is the most researched and practical book ever written on cell-group ministry! Joel traveled the globe to find out why certain churches and small groups are successful in reaching the lost. He freely shares the answer within this volume. If you are a pastor or a small group leader, you should devour this book! It will encourage you and give you simple, practical steps for dynamic small group life and growth. 152 pgs.

HOW TO BE A GREAT CELL GROUP COACH
Research has proven that the greatest contributor to cell group success is the quality of coaching provided for cell group leaders. Following in the footsteps of his bestselling book, *How to Lead a GREAT Cell Group Meeting,* Comiskey provides a comprehensive guide for coaching cell group leaders. Chapters include: What a Coach Does, Listening, Celebrating, Caring, Strategizing, Challenging, and more. This book will prepare your coaches to be great mentors, supporters, and guides to the cell group leaders they oversee.

Order Toll-Free from TOUCH Outreach Ministries
1-800-735-5865 • Order Online: www.cellgrouppeople.com

GROUP MEMBER EQUIPPING

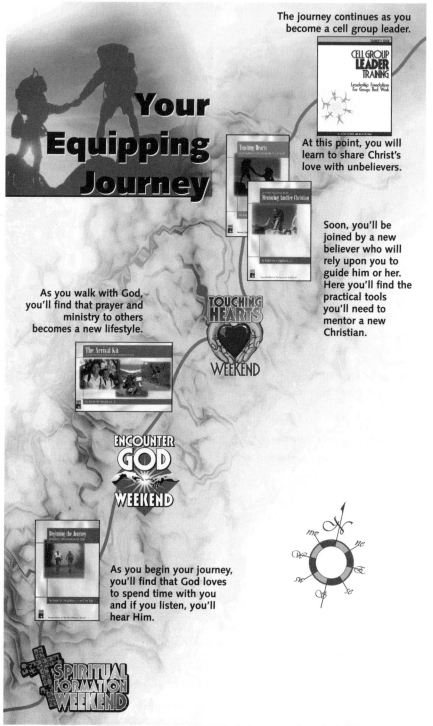

The journey continues as you become a cell group leader.

At this point, you will learn to share Christ's love with unbelievers.

Soon, you'll be joined by a new believer who will rely upon you to guide him or her. Here you'll find the practical tools you'll need to mentor a new Christian.

As you walk with God, you'll find that prayer and ministry to others becomes a new lifestyle.

As you begin your journey, you'll find that God loves to spend time with you and if you listen, you'll hear Him.

CELL GROUP LEADER TRAINING RESOURCES

CELL GROUP LEADER TRAINING:
by Scott Boren and Don Tillman

The *Trainer's Guide* and *Participant's Manual* parallel the
teaching of Comiskey's *How to Lead a Great Cell Group
Meeting*. Through the use of teaching, creative activities,
small group interaction, and suggested between-the-
training exercises, this eight-session training will prepare
people for cell group leadership like no other tool. The
Trainer's Guide provides teaching outlines for all eight
sessions and options for organizing the training,
including different weekly options and retreat options.
The *Trainer's Guide* also has bonus sections, including
teaching outlines for the *Upward, Inward, Outward, Forward* Seminar and detailed
interview discussion guides for *The Journey Guide for Cell Group Leaders*. This
comprehensive training tool will establish your group leaders on a sure foundation.

HOW TO LEAD A GREAT CELL GROUP MEETING
by Joel Comiskey

Joel Comiskey takes you beyond theory and into the "practical tips of
the trade" that will make your cell group gathering vibrant! This
hands-on guide covers all you need to know, from basic how-to's of
getting the conversation started to practical strategies for dynamic
ministry times. If you're looking to find out what really makes a cell
group meeting great…this book has the answers! 144 pgs.

8 HABITS OF EFFECTIVE SMALL GROUP LEADERS
by Dave Earley

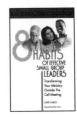

Are your cell leaders truly effective in changing lives? They can be!
After years of leading and overseeing growing small groups, Pastor
Dave Earley has identified 8 core habits of effective leaders. When
adopted, these habits will transform your leadership too. The habits
include: Dreaming • Prayer • Invitations • Contact Preparation •
Mentoring • Fellowship • Growth. When your leaders adopt and
practice these habits, your groups will move from once-a-week
meetings to an exciting lifestyle of ministry to one another and the
lost! 144 pgs.

LEADING FROM THE HEART
by Michael Mack

Recharge your cell leadership! Powerful cell leaders share a common
trait: a passionate heart for God. They know their priorities and know
that time with Him is always at the top of the list. This book will renew
leaders' hearts, refocus their priorities and recharge their ministry. If
you have a sense that your leaders are tired of ministry or frustrated
with people, this title will help! And, if your leaders have great
attitudes and you want to help them move to the next level, this book
will move them into new fields, white for harvest! 152 pgs.

ADDITIONAL CELL GROUP LEADER RESOURCES

TURNING MEMBERS INTO LEADERS
by Dave Earley

The development of new cell leaders is the key to growing cell groups. The best way to raise up new leaders is through mentoring current cell group members within cell groups. Pastor Dave Earley has observed that cell leaders employ some basic steps when successfully raising up new leaders. The steps include Dream • Demonstrate • Discover • Deepen • Describe • Determine • Develop • Deploy. When current cell group leaders use these simple steps in mentoring future leaders, they will discover that their ministries are multiplied and new cell group started.

UPWARD, INWARD, OUTWARD, FORWARD WORKBOOK
by Jim Egli

This easy to use workbook, combined with the facilitator's presentation (included in *Cell Group Leader Training: Trainer's Guide*) will help your cell groups grow in the four basic dynamics of healthy cell life. Upward: Deepening your relationship to the Father; Inward: Deepening community between cell members; Outward: Reaching the lost for Jesus successfully; Forward: Developing and releasing new leaders. 72 pgs.

THE JOURNEY GUIDE FOR CELL GROUP LEADERS
This tool will help your interns and cell leaders evaluate their leadership abilities and determine their next steps toward effective group leadership. It will help you as a pastor or trainer identify the needs of your future or current leaders so that you can better train and mentor them.

303 ICEBREAKERS
You will never need another icebreaker book. This collection places at your fingertips easy-to-find ideas divided into nine categories, such as "Including the Children," "When a Visitor Arrives" and "Lighthearted and Fun." This is a needed reference for every cell meeting. We've included instructions on how to lead this part of the meeting effectively. 156 pgs.

OUR BLESSING LIST POSTER

Growing cell churches have proven that constant prayer for the lost yields incredible results! Use this nifty poster to list the names of your *oikos* and pray for them every time you meet. 34" x 22", folds down to 8.5" x 11" and comes with a handout master, equipping track and a master prayer list. Pack of 10.

ARE YOU FISHING WITH A NET?
by Randall G. Neighbour

Lead your group into team evangelism. These proven steps will prepare your members to reach out effectively as a group. 12 pgs.

Order Toll-Free from TOUCH® Outreach Ministries
1-800-735-5865 • Order Online: www.cellgrouppeople.com

CELL GROUP VISION BOOKS

MAKING CELL GROUPS WORK
by M. Scott Boren
This book breaks down the transition process into eight manageable parts. If your church is just beginning its transition, these materials will help you focus on building cells on a sure foundation. If you are in the midst of developing cell groups, it highlights where to focus your energy. No matter where you are with your church, these resources will help you identify your current stage of cell development and articulate a plan to address that stage.

THE SECOND REFORMATION
by William A. Beckham
Don't jump head-first into a cell church transition or church plant without reading this book! Beckham brilliantly walks you through the logic of a cell/celebration structure from a biblical and historical perspective. He provides you with a step-by-step strategy for launching your first cells. This wonderful companion to Neighbour's material will ground you in the values and vision necessary for a successful transition to cells. 253 pgs.

WHERE DO WE GO FROM HERE? THE 10TH ANNIVERSARY EDITION
by Ralph W. Neighbour, Jr.
With updated data on new cell church models, new information on equipping and harvest events and practical teaching on how to begin a transition, this book will continue to stir hearts to dream about what the church can be. You will find hope for the church in North America and discover the new things that Dr. Neighbour has learned over the last 10 years. Share this vision with a friend. 400 pgs.

THE SHEPHERD'S GUIDEBOOK
by Ralph W. Neighbour, Jr.
With over 100,000 copies in print, this tested guide will equip and train your leaders to develop community and lead people into relationship evangelism, by learning to listen to God's voice on behalf of their flock. Cell leaders will gain tools for leading a cell meeting, and learn pastoring skills that will multiply the ministry of your church. 256 pages.

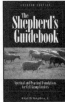

LIFE IN HIS BODY
by David Finnell
Communicate the vision of the cells to everyone in your church with this simple tool. The short chapters followed by discussion questions clearly define cell life for your leaders and members so that they can catch a lifestyle of prayer, community and evangelism. This book will give your church hope and vision as your members discover the possibilities of the New Testament community. 160 pgs.

Order Toll-Free from TOUCH® Outreach Ministries
1-800-735-5865 • Order Online: www.cellgrouppeople.com

Make Cell Groups Work Online!

Our website was designed for pastors just like you!

Free articles from *CellChurch Magazine* & *CellGroup Journal.*

Fast and secure online resource purchases.

Watch a streaming video on the cell movement.

Discover other churches with cell groups in your area or denomination.

Post your resume or search for a new staff member in our cell-based classifieds area.

Free downloads of leader's guides, presentations, and software to track cell growth.

Interact with other pastors and experts in our bulletin board forum.

What are you waiting for?

Grab a cup of coffee and visit us now...

www.cellgrouppeople.com